D1299977

TODAY'S INSPIRED LATINA™

Volume X

LIFE STORIES OF SUCCESS IN THE FACE OF ADVERSITY

JACQUELINE S. RUIZ

Today's Inspired Latina Volume X

© Copyright 2022, Fig Factor Media, LLC.
All rights reserved.

This book is a compilation of stories from numerous people who have each contributed a chapter and is designed to provide inspiration to our readers.

It is sold with the understanding that the publisher and the individual authors are not engaged in the rendering of psychological, legal, accounting or other professional advice. The content and views in each chapter are the sole expression and opinion of its author and not necessarily the views of Fig Factor Media, LLC.

For more information, contact:

Fig Factor Media, LLC | www.figfactormedia.com
Today's Inspired Latina | www.todayslatina.com

Cover Design & Layout by Juan Pablo Ruiz

Printed in the United States of America

ISBN: 978-1-957058-39-9
Library of Congress Number: 2022935783

I want to dedicate this very special tenth volume of *Today's Inspired Latina* to the almost 250 authors who have poured their hearts and trust into the series. Each one of you have paved the way while believing in me, in this mission, and this community. Thank you for the beauty and the magix we have created together since 2014.

Table of Contents:

Acknowledgments 6

Preface by Edith Lopez 7

Introduction by Jacqueline S. Ruiz 10

AUTHOR CHAPTERS

DR. ANITZA SAN MIGUEL.. 13

MARIA HERRERA PALOMA 23

DALIA GONZALEZ 35

MARTHA RAZO... 45

DR. ALICIA LA HOZ... 55

NANCY C. VASSER 65

NATALIA C. FRANCO.. 75

LORENA MARTINEZ.. 85

ERICA PRISCILLA SANDOVAL, LCSW 95

LUZY D KING 105

ANA LARREA-ALBERT 113

ROCIO ALEJANDRA CARROLL 123

SANDRA KEYS 133

ISABEL RAMIREZ 141

MONICA RIVERS 151

ANDREA MORALES 163

MARÍA DEL CARMEN IBARRA ZEPEDA 173

CRISTINA FLORES 185

DINORAH GÓMEZ 197

AMARANTA GAYTAN 205

SALLY DELGADO , M.ED. 217

LORENA REBECA BELTRÁN GONZÁLEZ 225

About the Author 234

Acknowledgments

First of all, I'd like to thank everyone in the Fig Factor Media Team.

Thank you to Gabriela Hernández Franch, for your amazing dedication to this book series and to Izar Olivares who has been supporting us as the newest team member. You ladies rock! Manuel Serna, I appreciate your work very much! Juan Pablo Ruiz, the most talented creative director and partner I could have! Jessica Galvan for giving her magic through the editing process for this very significant volume. Karen Dix, who in the beginning, brainstormed with me over thirty different possible book titles and was the editor throughout most of the series. Irene Anzola for her project management skills and *"corrección de estilo"* for the Spanish volumes and all the love she has put into this project throughout the years. I am immensely grateful for everyone.

- JACQUELINE S. RUIZ

Preface

ADMIRATION MOVES HEARTS

This book would not have reached my hands without the generosity of Jacqueline Camacho, with whom I will always be grateful for the gift of allowing me to take a small part of this tenth volume of inspiring stories of women distinguished by their courage and their enthusiasm to live.

This leads me to think about the number of perfection: 10. But at the same time, I ponder on how we don't, nor should, know everything. It cost me, but I learned that 10 means excellence and that seeking perfection brings fatigue with it. However, by giving our best effort we can calm our hearts. Excellence is a way to live with greater joy, but it is not a final goal. No one comes out from a familiar place and goes aboard into a new and unknown one without feeling uneasiness or disorientation.

In a beautiful game of mirrors and reflections, while reading the stories, I felt a clear and true personal identification with experiences like those I have lived. Breaking a pattern to build a better life is an important step, something I went through as well. One woman takes this step and, after her, another one follows. Soon a strength and support chain, a possibility, is built. This message transmits to others that dreams can come true but that also at times we have emotions and conflicts inside that vibrate at the slightest provocation.

The authors of these stories add value today by simply

sharing them. They have awareness of their lives and serve others. They know their power. I could sense that through their words, with a smile of admiration upon my face. Although the mountain is high and seems very far away, with courage, discipline, and self-love you can get there too. And not only that, but you can allow your soul to be excited with every step.

Being alive is a journey that is given to us. What we do with it makes the difference.

That's why I am so grateful for Jacqueline's gift in all its worth. We came to this world to grow. We were given a precious opportunity for expansion. Knowing that, if you can have courage, bravery, and prowess to thrive while inviting others to believe and grow, that is the master opportunity of this journey.

Entanglement between the women in this book occurs naturally, like a magnet. The facts disappear, but the lesson remains. Who has not experienced imposter syndrome? Doubting is a right. Doubting that we can go forward in our inner strength is valid. Yet, to continue moving despite the lack of absolute certainty is a sign that our feet are strong and that our heart is the best compass to orient us.

Women are taking a quantum leap worldwide. From defending their individual rights so they can recognize their worth, to look beyond their circumstances. The lives of the women in this compendium support and multiply this feast of conscience and self-love. Thank you for choosing me to raise a joyful cheer of *Long Live Women!* To those who live life as an opportunity to always be on time to jump to a more luminous reality, more projective, more in line with the evolution of consciousness.

The learnings mark us. They leave an indelible spot that shows us pieces of what we were and what we will live. How can we not be moved by small acts from ordinary people with extraordinary results? Living a common life, an everyday life, is fine and no one would say otherwise, but how can we take the great leap of believing in ourselves and launch to conquer other fields of learning? The term "eternal learner" resonates with me and will continue to create harmony in every interaction with an opportunity of support, expansion and faith. Everyone decides how much they can expand their wings, to what extent they can open paths and help others. There are no limits when our trust shines like a lamp within us.

Doing things differently and daring to fly towards better opportunities is always a good idea. Especially with the right to be yourself and without hurting anyone. Behind stay our ancestors—the origin from which we started walking one day with a suitcase full of dreams and illusions. A world of dreams opens before us and perhaps we tremble at the possibility of not doing the right thing. But in the how lay the strategies, the ways each one of us will use to conquer the top of the mountain. And once you arrive you greet the world and yell: You can do it too!

Edith Lopez
Soul Path Coach

Introduction

This is the tenth and final volume of *Today's Inspired Latina*. I want to close this series with a beautiful bow and a significant look back at all the magic that has taken place.

Today's Inspired Latina has made countless connections and thousands of powerful micro moments. We've had book launches with 300-800 people making for historic events within our community. We have received support from some of the most influential brands like Estee Lauder engraving over 600 lipsticks and three separate events hosted in the New York Times building. *Today's Inspired Latina* catapulted countless other projects that took on a life of its own. LATINATalks which recorded over 160 talks of our contributing authors throughout the years, and who inspired Young LATINATalks and three different volumes of *Today's Inspired Young Latina* and even the *Today's Inspired Leader* the series. The amazing list of book titles sprouting from Today's Inspired Latina continues with *The Word Power series, Latinas in Aviation, Latinas in Architecture, Latinas Rising Up in HR, Latinas in Social Work, Latinas in Real Estate, Hispanic Star Rising, and Mujeres de HACE, and many more!* All of these books totaling almost 900 stories, primarily from Latinas, have been shared because of the amazing phenomenon that is *Today's Inspired Latina*. It feels incredible to pave the way for so many women.

It makes me emotional to think this will be the final volume of *Today's Inspired Latina*, but I am looking forward to shifting my efforts to supporting the community we have built and creating more magix while forming amazing partnerships around the world. There is so much more in store.

I am beyond grateful, completely humbled, and appreciative of all the magix this series has brought to my life. I have tried to give it all back in as many ways as I could through guidance and divine downloads. When I receive a divine download, even if it makes no business sense, I completely surrender to it and that always leads me to a beautiful and amazing result. For example, we didn't charge a penny to attend the MAGIX retreats and even paid for travel and hotel for some of the attendees because of a divine download.

When you follow your heart, listen to God's whispers, and serve other people while living with a higher frequency of love—anything is possible. If one reader gets inspired, or finds a connection they didn't have before, or one more life is saved because they believed there was something greater for them— then I have done my job. That is what I hope for all ten volumes of *Today's Inspired Latina* to continue to live out. That is the legacy I want to share with the world.

Jacqueline S. Ruiz
Entrepreneur, Author, Speaker,
Philanthropist, Pilot
Founder of Today's Inspired Latina

Dr. Anitza San Miguel

"Everything is possible in life. All you have to do is trust, believe, and take action."

Growing up in Puerto Rico with parents who never attended college, I didn't have many professional scientists in my life to look up to, but in my heart, I knew becoming a scientist was part of my grand search for meaning in life.

I dreamt of becoming a neurosurgeon, but God revealed a different path. With the support and guidance of many incredible mentors and my family, I pursued a bachelor's degree in Biology, quickly rising to the top of my class and accepting an internship at the National Institutes of Health (NIH). I continued to follow my passion for science and obtained a master's degree in Biotechnology from John Hopkins University.

Though the formal education was rigorous, I found the personal growth and challenges along the way even more intense. As one of the few Latinas in the group, I was constantly facing stereotypes and being met with skepticism that required me to continuously work to prove myself to others.

After completing my master's degree in Biotechnology, I began teaching Biology at a community college, where I discovered that I was just as passionate about helping others grow as I was about being in the lab with cells, microscopes and pipettes. With this realization that I could merge my love for science and education, I began pursuing my doctorate in Higher Education Administration while working full time. I was finally on the path to becoming aligned with my true passions in life.

It wasn't long before I found myself at home with my husband amid a full-blown panic attack. I received an email from my dissertation chair at the time. It was the end of the month and I had to make sure that I submitted my case quota for the end of the month. All my efforts to break the glass ceiling pursuing grad school and facing mounting pressures at work were piling up. It hit me that I wasn't as happy as I knew I could be.

My life transitioned again as I left my full-time job to focus on school and my family. After the birth of my daughter, I obtained my doctorate and began work as a faculty member at a local community college. Although I was pursuing what I thought was my passion, I found myself outside of my comfort zone. I faced surprising challenges that helped me develop as an educator. I was in my third year as full-time faculty when I was appointed as interim Associate Dean due to a campus organizational restructure. I was excited about the opportunity and rose to the challenge. However, the appointment didn't sit well with some faculty who had been at the college longer than me. It was a very stressful work environment. I was constantly checking emails and working long hours. In addition, my husband traveled for weeks at a time for work. There were many times that

I felt like a single mom. I had four babysitters that would help me with my daughter. I am certainly not the first mom in this situation. The guilt of not being there for my daughter at times haunted me. At one point, I felt my professional and personal lives were upside down. I felt like an imposter.

It was at this moment that I made the decision to step back, reflect and evaluate. I accepted a new job in Florida and began my intentional growth journey. My purpose began to crystallize. Over the past years, I uncovered that what I truly love is adding value to the lives of others through assisting them in discovering and unleashing their unlimited potential.

MY FATHER'S WORDS

It's Monday, October 25, 2021. As I wait to board my flight to San Juan, Puerto Rico, an eerie feeling of *nostalgia* and gratitude take over my mind. Every time I travel, I think about my dad working in the cargo division. The only airline my dad traveled is the one I'm about to board; American Airlines.

I start thinking back to when I received an acceptance letter to do a one-year internship at the National Institutes of Health in Bethesda, Maryland. I was so excited and, at the same time, scared because it was my first time living by myself. No *'mami* or *papi'* around to take care of me. Although I considered myself independent, I didn't think my parents were prepared for me to leave them for a higher purpose.

I clearly remember the days leading up to the moment I left. I told my parents I was only doing the internship and then I was coming back. One year, that's it. As I was getting some things ready in the living room my dad, with a firm voice said to me, "Anitza, prepare yourself and study. Because the day that you have to *"mandar un hombre a 'freír espárragos'* (send a man to get lost), you can take your things and go." Wow! What just happened here? I was in shock. What did my dad just say? Why did he tell me this? My dad was a man of a very few words. He would hardly share his opinion with you. But, when he spoke, you better listen carefully. He never expressed himself that way. This was not a "normal" conversation that I had with my dad. He wanted me to have the education that he did not have.

It wouldn't be until after he passed away that I found, amongst his belongings, a letter from a junior college in New York City offering him a scholarship. The fact that my dad could have earned a degree left me feeling sad and proud. Sad because he never shared with me that he earned a scholarship. Proud because he had the potential to be, do, and have anything he wanted in his life, but life circumstances and other things that I would never know, didn't allow him to complete a college degree. His path could have been different if he had attended college. Now, I fully understand why my dad empowered me to be, do, and have what I want in my life. He empowered me to always excel, to be resilient, and to be independent. He empowered me to be in control of my life.

When I left Puerto Rico for the internship, my oldest cousin drove me to the airport. My mom, dad, and brother were working. I guess no one wanted to say goodbye. I now believe that they were avoiding this hard moment.

I was quietly waiting for my flight in the airport and thinking about what I was about to do. I boarded the plane with a heart full of emotions. I sat on the right side of the plane at the window seat holding back my tears. I was staring outside still holding my tears when I saw my dad driving the cargo car (the ones that the airlines use to put all the luggage to the plane). He was waving trying to figure out where I was seated. I waved back. I couldn't hold back my tears anymore. This was real. I was leaving Puerto Rico. I was leaving my family behind. It's just me now.

What was I doing? Who will wait for me at the airport in Maryland? Who will wake me up in the morning? I had so many questions, and no immediate answers.

As the plane started moving, so did my dad, waving goodbye with a big smile on his face. He was proud that *"la nena"* (his little girl) was pursuing her dream.

I left the island that day for what was supposed to be a year and it turned into twenty-four years. I have been back on multiple occasions to visit family and used to travel every year. Now my mom lives closer to me in Florida so I don't get back as often as I'd like.

On this day, I go back to be with family as my uncle has passed away. He was my dad's cousin. Those emotions that I had put away emerged today as I sat in the plane writing. It's time to unload and unleash. Time to heal. It is time to close a chapter in my life so that my unlimited potential can be set free.

LIMITING BELIEFS ARE REAL

I sometimes wondered what the specific time in my life was where I started to be a perfectionist. Growing up, I was always

17

well dressed for the casual Fridays at school. In elementary school, I used to wear dresses that were made just for me (*de puntillas*). Oh, and don't forget the shoes! I had every single color of shoes.

Since both of my parents worked full-time, my brother and I had a baby-sitter that became our second family. Her kids (now adults) were like my brothers. They took my brother and I to basketball games. My second mom, as I used to call her, was a seamstress and her husband worked at a shoe store. I was the daughter that they didn't have (they had three boys). Her husband used to bring me a new pair of shoes every week. Lucky me! I think this is where my love for shoes started.

In college, I remember going to see my Chemistry professor during his office hours for tutoring. There were other students in his office chatting with him. My professor was telling everyone "jokingly" how much he was charging each of them for tutoring. When I entered the room, I asked him, "What about me?" He said, "For you, it's ten dollars the hour." I said, "Ten dollars, why?" His response took me by surprise. He said, "Look at the way you dress. You can afford ten dollars per hour." Bingo! This is when my limiting beliefs started to be programmed. The beliefs of scarcity, self-doubt and self-image set in. What would others say? Did I dress too much or too little? If I dress nicely, are people going to think that I am snobby? Comments like the one my professor made can make you or break you. In my case, it broke me. I started to play small.

It has taken me years to recognize that I was playing small. I used to say "I'm under the radar. I'm staying behind the scenes."

Why? Why would I do that to myself? God created me perfectly and abundantly as I am. Why would I play small? It's the limiting beliefs that were holding me back from being who I was created to be.

It wasn't until I began my intentional personal growth journey and started working with coaches that I learned that I must be me and not what others want me to do. I don't have to be what society dictates a woman should be. I must be me!

I learned that I must live my dream and not someone else's dream. I learned that I have big dreams and therefore I need to play BIG.

PERFECTIONISM. IS IT GOOD OR BAD?

As part of my journey, I discovered how perfectionism was holding me back. Every time I started a personal or professional project, I had to have everything, absolutely everything clear as water. I needed to know all the details...the whole story before I started. Has this happened to you?

This habit of needing everything perfect led me to stress, anxiety, and taking all the time in the world. What was supposed to take me a few minutes or a few hours, took me weeks or months. In an attempt to have everything perfect, many times I gave up.

I remember one of my mentors telling me, "Anitza, you have to suspend the requirement to know how, let the how be revealed." Say what? *Horror!* How could I suspend the requirement to know everything? I need to know everything. "Impossible," I said, "I can't miss a single detail." It took me time to understand my mentor's words. Today, I can say that I have learned to suspend the need to know everything. It has been a process. Pursuing perfection paralyzes.

How many times have you started something and not finished it because it is not totally perfect?

I learned that I need to act every day, small steps at a time rather than sitting comfortably and waiting for divine intervention. Yes, God is going to help me, and I also need to help myself. I need to do the work. I need to act. I learned to trust in myself. Trust that I am fully resourced to be, do, and have what I want in my life. I have learned to believe. I believe in my skills, knowledge, abilities, giftedness, and intelligence.

When doubt, fear, and perfectionism pay me a visit (and they often do) I challenge each of them with an I AM statement. I am strong. I am unique. I am perfect. I am intelligent. I am a leader. I am worthy. I am resilient. I am abundant. I am love. I am happy. I AM ME!

REFLECTION QUESTIONS

1. What are the limiting beliefs that are holding you back from unleashing your unlimited potential?

2. Where are you now and where are you heading?

3. How many times have you started something and didn't finish because it wasn't perfect?

BIOGRAPHY

Dr. Anitza San Miguel is a transformational leadership coach, scientist, and passionate educator who helps leaders unleash their full potential without limitations. She has more than 20 years of experience in research and education, where she has served as a science professor and dean at institutions in Virginia and Florida. She has also worked at the National Institutes of Health (NIH) and the U.S. Patent and Trademark Office. Growing up in Puerto Rico with parents who never attended college, Dr. San Miguel didn't have many professional scientists in her life to look up to, but in her heart she knew becoming a scientist was meant to be a part of her life journey. With the support and guidance of many incredible mentors, she pursued a bachelor's degree in biology and a master's degree in biotechnology. She later merged her love for science and education, obtaining her doctorate in higher education administration while working full time.

Dr. San Miguel currently serves as dean leading a college team in Orlando, Florida and as the owner and coach of ASM Mentors, LLC. When she is not working, she enjoys savoring quality time with her husband and 13-year-old daughter, traveling, and journaling.

Dr. Anitza San Miguel
anitza@anitzasanmiguel.com
IG: @anitza21
LinkedIn: /anitza-sanmiguel

BREAKING WITH TRADITION IS A VERY GOOD THING

Maria Herrera Paloma

"In learning you will teach, and in teaching you will learn."
- Phil Collins

I was born into a large Mexican Catholic family and at four years old, I arrived in Chicago. I was following the traditional path, where the expectation was, I would go to college, get married and start a family, and then stay home to raise my children. For all intents and purposes, I was right on track to live the traditional life of a typical "modern" Mexican woman. I had a fierce understanding of what I wanted and what I didn't want. Most of the time I wasn't afraid to voice it. This sometimes created tension between me and my older siblings or other family members.

Still, there was always a slight doubt or fear on my part to go against tradition. Even though it was acceptable to attend college, I was still expected to eventually marry and raise a family. I knew I wanted to go to college, and I wanted a career. I knew I also wanted a family but I didn't want to be married with a house full of kids at a very young age. That path was just not for me. Some family members didn't quite understand that. I did go to college, Loyola University, and maintained tradition by commuting and not going away to school. I met my husband my freshman year, we married three years after graduation and waited three years before starting a family.

My husband had a very good career and we were blessed with the opportunity for me to stay home to raise our three children. Of course, there were naysayers, "Entonces para qué fue a college; para quedarse en casa con los hijos!" But I knew that this was the best thing for my children, and I also knew my college degree would always be in my back pocket as a backup in the future. I became a stay-at-home mom and ten years later, I began feeling like I wanted and could do more. For this reason, I returned to school at forty years old to earn a Masters of Arts in Teaching and became a Dual Language classroom teacher.

IN SEARCH OF A MUCH BIGGER CLASSROOM

As a self-identified "lifelong learner", I have always made a conscientious effort to stay current on trends and issues that impact the Latino community. I soon realized the glaring disparities regarding health and wealth that continue to take a huge toll on Latinos. While there were many programs that were accessible to the community, there wasn't much offered to our Spanish-speaking community. The first initiative I decided to address was health, so I took the plunge and at fifty years old, became a certified Yoga Instructor. My goal was to teach Yoga en Español in my community. I conducted classes for students and moms and both were extremely well-received. I was filled with love and pride. I was so proud of myself for taking a "leap with

Faith" and now I was helping my community in an important and unique way. I had accomplished my first goal and was excited for all that was coming my way. I had always loved practicing yoga and now I was able to share my love with others.

I was starting to find my voice. I had already been surrounded by many strong women; my mother, three sisters and a slew of nieces who supported me in my family life. I made it a priority to further surround myself with empowered women who mentored me in other areas. My faith had grown stronger with the help of my sister Silvia, who is a devout Catholic. She encouraged me then, and still encourages me today, to stay true to my values and beliefs. However, the women I was meeting now were supporting me in my personal growth and my professional growth. Becoming more focused on my health was also becoming more important. As I sought new professional ventures these women were the ones who motivated me, held me accountable, and pushed me to be brave to step out of my comfort zone. As I led more yoga classes, I realized that teaching was becoming a passion and I started to feel more empowered to find other ways to help my community.

AN OPEN MIND PROPELS ME TO DISCOVER MY PURPOSE

I began delving into the financial arena and I came across jarring research that said "more than half of Americans (or 51 percent) have less than three months' worth of expenses covered in an emergency fund, according to Bankrate's July 2021 Emergency Savings Survey....1 in 4 Americans (or 25 percent) indicate having no emergency fund at all—up from 21 percent in 2020."* In addition, about 46% of Americans do not have life insurance to cover final expenses.** Even further, statistics show that 64% of Americans either feel their savings are not on track or aren't sure they are financially ready for retirement.*** And these statistics only grew more dire during the pandemic for everyone, but especially for people of color and for Hispanic communities everywhere.

We saw the rise in GoFundMe pages when so many people were losing loved ones during the pandemic. It was especially disheartening to learn that even though this crowdfunding platform helped so many, there were still people not receiving enough funds to support their families during a very difficult time. A recent New York Times article ("The Inequality of the GoFundMe Economy" by Shira Ovide) stated: "It's a problem that so many Americans have to resort to internet donations to meet basic needs like food, housing and medical attention."

This knowledge propelled me to continue researching and find out if there was anything that could alleviate this situation, and I learned of a platform, World Financial Group, that does just that. Their mission is to empower families with financial literacy education so they may learn how to work toward financial stability, build a legacy and create real generational wealth. I took a huge leap of faith and became a business owner. This was another example of me stepping out of my comfort zone. I had been very interested in the financial industry for a long time but was still not feeling confident in sharing the knowledge

I had. Learning of this company and the tremendous amount of training, support, collaboration and camaraderie that existed within helped me decide that this was the exact next step for me. I knew this was the next goal for me to continue my path as an educator but now it would be in the financial realm.

I am fully committed to my role as a teacher, instructor, mentor, and coach! My days are filled with class sessions, workshops, meetings, one on one phone calls and networking events! *I love it!* For now, I am a classroom teacher by day and a financial literacy specialist by night helping families learn how to plan and build stable financial futures for themselves and their children. My days are so full that I need a trusty calendar and a gazillion alarms on my phone to remind me of what's next. *(It drives my husband nuts!)*

Other days I make time for Yoga at home, family, organizing foundation work, coaching, and planning the classroom work for the week. My weeknights are also full of activities related to my business: attending or conducting networking events, phone calls, team meetings, business meetings, one-on-one meetings, workshops, training videos, and of course, the weekly yoga class I teach! My days are purposefully filled and productive. I arrive at the end of my days spent, but satisfied in knowing I am impacting people's lives in positive ways.

I have found my passion. I am an educator. I will be learning and teaching for the rest of my life and I can't wait. Along this half century of life, I have continuously honed my exceptional organizational skills, my love of numbers, and my enthusiasm for helping others. I am now so excited to continue to share this as my retirement from the Dual Language classroom is only a short four years away. At that time, I will be able to continue my journey and dedicate all my efforts and energy to continue building my financial coaching business with WFG.

CONTINUOUSLY BUILDING MY SELF-CONFIDENCE

"Be confident!" It's a statement I often say to many people. It took me a while to believe it for myself. It took me...oh...about 40+ years or so...to say it and to finally own it!

If you've only met me recently you would be utterly surprised at this fact. I was not always confident in my own skin, in my own thoughts, in my own beliefs, in my own reality. Would you say this is you? I know there are many who would agree with the statement: It takes us a while to believe in ourselves or our "selves". I could also share that while in college I was presented with a couple of opportunities that at the time seemed very challenging to me. One opportunity was with a newly formed organization, and it was for an internship that was not paid. At the time I needed a paying job so I turned it down. Today, that organization is large and flourishing.

For some time I felt regret not jumping on the opportunity but it was just not the right time for me. Today, I no longer feel this regret nor do I regret having taken so long to find myself. I am who I am now, because I've had a lot of wonderful, pivotal experiences with amazing mentors that have helped shape me and enabled me to grow. Do I wish I had started on this purposeful path sooner? Sometimes. But I cannot dwell on this "should have" moment. Rather, I choose to live in the "I am here" moment, and embracing it means I have arrived.

I have been on a road of discovery for the past 10 years or so. It has been a lot of work, but I feel I have undergone an immense transformation. I am comfortable in my own skin, in my gray hair, my wrinkled hands and the stretch marks that prove my motherhood. I sought out and found great mentors who guided me and supported me but I could not have had this great breakthrough without the consistent encouragement, caring and loving support from my husband of 31 years, Miguel! He has always been my rock, my biggest cheerleader and motivator. He's kept me accountable and grounded and I am extremely proud of the life we've created together.

Growing up and early in my career, I was faced with opportunities that I did not jump on because of thoughts of self-doubt, fear of failure, embarrassment, or fear of not knowing enough about a subject! For a long time, I also felt regret for not trying, for not stepping out of my comfort zone. Through finding love for myself, I began to separate from all that was becoming unhealthy for me. This meant people, even family members, as well as my own negative beliefs and poor habits—anything that kept me doubtful and fearful. I recall feeling a sense of betrayal, especially toward my family, but I soon learned it was more about self-acceptance and self-love. I used to joke that I was always a late bloomer, but in fact I really was. I am continuously growing but I feel like I have finally blossomed.

And this could very well be you! Know that when one door closes there will be others nearby that can be opened. But these can only be opened with courage and vulnerability on your part. Do not feel regret for the decisions you've made in your past. Embrace these as experiences that will help you in the future.

The most important lesson I can share with you today is to never stop learning, never stop searching, never stop looking for answers. Some people just know what their passion is from a very young age and for some of us it takes a little longer. Today I know that all the waiting, all the experiences, all the books, and people in my life have helped to map out a path. I know I started the journey of discovery "later in life". Becoming a classroom teacher was just the first steppingstone and I never stopped.

Finally, I hope that my story has impacted you to realize that it may take a while for you to find your passion, it may take a while for you to uncover and believe in your many gifts, but never stop looking. Be open to what others see in you. Believe when people tell you that you have a gift. Open the gift and share it with the world, whether you are twenty years young or forty years young. Never believe that your time is up…. Never stop learning because life never stops teaching! We are continuously a work in progress!

REFLECTION QUESTIONS

1. Have you ever struggled with the feeling that you are breaking cultural traditions? Do you struggle with a sense of disloyalty toward your culture and heritage when you feel the urge to go against these?

2. Has there been a time when you were faced with an opportunity you didn't take for fear of failure or embarrassment?

3. What are you passionate about?

BIOGRAPHY

When I share with others that I immigrated to Chicago at the age of 4, they often wonder if I am *"más Americana que Mexicana"* but this could not be further from the truth, given the fierce pride I have for my culture and its rich traditions. And now, at the age of 56, finally having my story told and I am in control of my own narrative. As my life reads like an open book, here is how it has unfolded:

Chapter 1: The Early Years - Arrived in Chicago at the age of 4 from San Luis Potosi, Mexico. Her family of 9 took up residence in a 2-bedroom apartment in Chicago's Uptown neighborhood.

Chapter 2: The Acculturation Years - Growing up a simultaneous bilingual, became a product of two cultures, always managing to find the best in both. Highlights: Loyola University Alum - BBA degree, Major: Human Resources

Chapter 3. Professional Journey - Started in corporate America as HR Generalist for an Educational Publisher. Huge learning curve but learned to acclimate to a diverse group of people and systems.

Chapter 4. Blessed to become a SAHM - Married Miguel Paloma in 1991 and became mom to 3 beautiful children -Sofia, Miguel and Sam, but was far from "stay at home mom" status, involvement included PTA, Book Fair coordinator, Cub Scout Troop leader, room mom, school event volunteer, lunch lady, seamstress for my own children, scrapbook maker, to name a few.

Chapter 5. A return to school and new profession - Return to school for Masters of Art in Teaching at age of 42 - became a bilingual resource teacher and later a dual language classroom teacher

Chapter 6. The love of Yoga becomes pivotal - Received Yoga instructor certification at the age of 50 in order to teach Yoga en Español in my community, a truly life changing experience, immersed self in all self awareness books: The Secret, The Alchemist, Mindset, the Four Agreements

Chapter 7. Empowered Women Empower Women - Became President of The Fig Factor Foundation and Coach in The W.I.S.E. community - devoured books by Brene Brown and John Maxwell

Chapter 8. A second career at 56 - Became a business owner and Financial Coach pursuing the passion for teaching others the importance of building familial wealth; most recent reads include Brene Brown's Atlas of the Heart, Playing Big, The Compound Effect, The Seat of the Soul

Chapter 9. Retirement *(not quite ready to write this chapter as there is lots of teaching left to do)*

I consider myself an agent of change. Today as a new business owner and a state licensed financial professional, the real impact I'll make will be in building a Holistic Wellness following that encompasses both the physical and mental wellbeing as well as financial stability and growth.

I'm ready to utilize all I've learned to benefit you.

Take it from me!

Maria Herrera Paloma
www.mariapaloma.com
(847) 691-5873

Dalia Gonzalez

"Find your purpose in life first and make giving back and helping others your next mission."

As a woman, I soon figured out the world had already set an expectation for me. Being a young girl, I set myself to a higher standard knowing how hard it would be growing up as a Latina. Having faced my fair share of challenges and experiences, I can say that I'm much wiser and stronger in all aspects of my life. I've spent twenty-two years in the wellness industry helping families and empowering women as a coach. Overcoming many battles as a full-time working mom of four children has inspired many to become a better version of themselves while learning ways to work their body, mind, and soul.

MY CHILDHOOD DEFINED MY CHARACTER

Coming from a small town in Puebla, Mexico, and six siblings, I noticed that I was unique or at least that's how my mom made me feel. She would always say to me, "You are so special. You're not like the other kids.". Those exact words made me powerful and gave me strength to overcome difficult times. In order for my siblings and I to attend private school in the city, my parents had to make a lot of sacrifices. Most students were coming from foreign countries such as Germany, Spain, and Lebanon. As the minority, my siblings and I were seen as different. This personal experience made me feel pride in my identity. I taught myself how to gain the respect of others. Whether that was confronting bullies or even fighting them if I had to. Life was preparing me for the next chapter in my story. When I was eleven my dad lost his job. His only option was to move to the United States to find work. Soon after, my mom joined him and decided to find work in the United States. This was a huge step for her as she became a working mother in a new country. Meanwhile, we stayed in Mexico with our grandfather, Heriberto. My older sister and I oversaw the house and my younger siblings. We were responsible for taking my siblings to school, riding public transportation, and budgeting our money. It was a lot.

THE WORLD THAT I KNEW CHANGED SO I DID TOO

When I was fifteen years old, we all moved to California to be with my parents. Those last years in Mexico helped me mature. I learned skills that I would utilize later in life. During this time, church was a big support for me and my family. We were in East L.A, in a home renting just one room, for my mom, siblings, and my grandfather who came with us from Mexico. Going to school in East L.A I saw a lot of gangs, drugs, and shootings. It was a struggle adjusting to a new country, a new language, and a new world. I was never asked if I wanted to move, I always pictured myself finishing my career and being successful in Mexico. The move hit me in a way that I would've never imagined. I was slowly losing a part of myself and turning into an introvert. My world had changed completely.

My sister and I played varsity soccer at James A. Garfield High School, where we graduated top of our class with honors. We had great mentors such as Professor Palacios and Escalante. They also helped us to get into an engineering camp in Cal Poly Pomona due to our good grades. I was starting to gain confidence and hope about earning scholarships and going to college. Unfortunately, our citizenship status in the U.S. would not allow us to apply to any university. I ended up going to a community college working a full-time job in order to pay tuition as a foreign student. At this time, my parents were divorced, so I had to help my mom raise my siblings. Soon, I started working and making progress climbing the corporate ladder thanks to an opportunity from one of my mentors and family friends, Hugo.

PLANNING MY LIFE BEFORE SOMEONE ELSE DOES

I was living the American Dream. At twenty-one years old, I bought my first home, made a good income and started a family. What could go wrong? A couple of years later, all the dreams and goals that I had were gone. I was barely making it, living paycheck to paycheck with no ambition, a low self-esteem, and with a four-year-old daughter that I couldn't even take care of. I began to get frustrated with my job. I was working long hours and doing my best everyday but the opportunity to grow never presented itself. I felt like a failure. At this point I asked God to give me a sign and show me the way. I was tired of living like this. I had no friends; I was miserable with myself and hurting everyone around me.

In May 2000, my opportunity to lose weight and start my own business arrived when I least expected it. Sharing the Herbalife Nutrition products and impacting others came naturally to me thanks to my results. A year after I was working my business full time, we sold our house in California and moved to Atlanta. My husband at that time agreed to let me go and start my business with the condition that he was not going to financially help me. He would stay in California to pay off all our debts and sell the house before moving with us to Atlanta. We were living in a basement; making sacrifices, but we knew it would take time and hard work to make the "American Dream". I was passionate and I felt alive again. My dreams came back, but with purpose. It was bigger than just me. I wanted to make an impact on people's lives by helping them gain good nutrition and a better quality of life while helping them make an extra income. I had lost thirty-five lbs. I was happy and working on my personal development to bring back that confident little girl I used to be. This was just the beginning of my journey as an entrepreneur. My goals were big and nothing was going to stop me. I was working nonstop to build my business and then my husband joined. Our sacrifices began to pay off. We went from that small basement to buying our first home in Atlanta. Life was good.

STRUGGLES AS A MOM, SPOUSE, AND BUSINESSWOMAN

Once I found out how to grow and build my business everything just came naturally. The sky was the limit. After my second year full-time in the business, my second child was born. The next year, I was once again pregnant with my third. One of the reasons I joined this specific business was to have the flexibility to work while being present for my three children. While it was a huge blessing, deep inside I felt I was not doing my best as a mom, spouse, and entrepreneur. I had three kids and a team that depended on me to teach them how to build their business. Right then, I had to decide whether to use my kids as an excuse or a reason to keep growing. Once again, I made the choice to move again. This time to Mexico temporarily to look for a babysitter to help me so that I could focus on my business. I was still breastfeeding my six-month old baby when we moved. At this time, my marriage and spiritual life weren't a priority. I was just working to cover everyone's needs. Eventually, everything collapsed and I felt empty. I was distant from God when I needed guidance and had no direction in my personal life. Although I was achieving goals in my business and traveling to different cities and countries to share my successful story, I felt alone. My husband and I grew apart with no goals in common outside of our three children. A couple years later, in 2010 we got divorced.

DISCOVERING MY PURPOSE IN LIFE

Everyone had high expectations for me as a strong woman who knew what she wanted with a successful career. But I was struggling in my personal life. I was fragile and always putting on a mask so that no one would know that I was hurting inside. I got married again thinking that falling in love would make me happy. During my second marriage I learned more about myself than ever. I got to know the real me. I grew closer to God. I really wanted my marriage to work so I stopped doing the things that I loved to make time for us. In society, it was still strange to see a woman as the head of household and a man being a stay-at-home dad. At church, one of the leaders questioned why I traveled alone (business travels) and not with my husband. All the church ladies were stay at home moms, so I was the exception and viewed as different. I wanted to fit in, so I decided to abandon my business activities. Meanwhile, my husband's insecurities showed up and quickly turned into mental abuse. My self-esteem was completely gone. I felt like a horrible mom and wife.

Then, I got pregnant with my fourth child in 2015. I was so depressed and felt unloved. I was ashamed to tell anyone how I truly felt, including my own family. When my baby, Luna, was born, I suffered from postpartum depression. I felt imprisoned in my house with a newborn. My older kids knew things were not right in my marriage, so they quickly became my biggest support.

PAIN MAKES YOU GROW

I won that battle and came back with more confidence, knowing who I was and my worth. It was a hard decision to make but I got divorced again in 2018. I felt like I'd be judged and subjecting my older kids to a second divorce was not easy.

I couldn't make someone else happy and forget about my own happiness. Now, my daughter, Luna, is six years old. My oldest child, Dalis, is twenty-five, Jr is eighteen, and Milo is seventeen. They all are my biggest blessings and my motivation. I don't regret anything. My experiences made me the woman I am now. My kids are worth it, and their dads are men that came into my life to teach me lessons at the time. Now I have a great coparenting relationship with both. Jesus, my first ex-husband is still my business partner. We have such a great relationship that people still can't believe how well we get along. I also have a great co-parenting relationship with Luna's dad. This provides my kids confidence and security.

TIME TO GIVE BACK

I'm in a happy place enjoying being a full time and present mom for my four beautiful kids. I'm their number one fan at all their sports and activities. I love doing my business at my own pace without competing against anyone. But most importantly, I'm happy with myself. God is the center of my life and finally, after taking care of everyone else, I now put myself first.

After all my personal and professional experiences, I find myself having this incredible connection to empower people, especially women. Now my passion is to give women tools and guidance on how to be a better leader at home, in their community, congregation, work or business. I've had a successful business for twenty-two years while being a 1% top earner for Herbalife Nutrition. I'm a successful speaker and trainer in my industry, having the respect and admiration of many leaders. I'm the Founder Dalia y Asociados, D|G Team and now a formal JMT member. I'm always looking to become a better version of myself and give back to others while showing them what's possible if they're willing to do the work.

REFLECTION QUESTIONS

1. What helped build your character when you were a child?

2. What have you done to love yourself throughout the years?

3. Have you found your purpose in life?

BIOGRAPHY

Dalia Gonzalez is an ingenious, visionary entrepreneur and top one percent earner at Herbalife Nutrition. She has dedicated her life's work to empower others by keeping them out of their comfort zone, in order to unlock their maximum potential, especially in Latina women.

At a very young age, Dalia learned to build character, discipline and emotional intelligence while still in Mexico. Dalia eventually made it to East Los Angeles just in time to finish high school and graduated top of her class with honors by the hand of great mentors and professors like Jaime Escalante. Unable to attend college due to migratory status she pursued many opportunities in the work force and came across one that changed her life. In 2000 she joined the leading nutritional supplements company in the world, and since 2006 has now been an executive top one percent owner with business in over 8 countries with exponential growth year by year. She has also been involved in many businesses inside and outside of the U.S including health and wellness protein bars, real estate, keynote speaking, podcasts, personal development seminars, financial education, and youth leadership. Dalia is also very passionate about international travel, youth outreach, women's rights, DACA, equal rights and immigration reform.

In 2008 she was recognized in the Mundo Hispánico newspaper as the Latina that's breaking the rules in regards to the success of her business and breaking stereotypes. In 2015-2017 Dalia was also recognized for achieving the highest royalty growth in the U.S industry with Herbalife. More recently in these past 10 years she has been an Annual Mark Hughes Bonus Winner internationally. Today, she is committed to expand and share her success story to many women and help empower them to push them to be the best version of themselves.

Dalia looks forward to soon launching her own brand and becoming an author of her own book one day.

Dalia Gonzalez
https://daliagonzalez.com/
Instagram: @daliagonzalezint
Email: gonzalezdalia1@hotmail.com

Martha Razo

"Set your goals so high they call you crazy."

I was born in Michoacan, Mexico and lived there for my first year of life. My parents came to the United States seeking the glamorous and promising American dream. They left their parents behind, their home, their customs, and the best tacos. They wanted their Martita to go to college to become a working professional and for us to have better living conditions. My parents later had my brother and best friend, Rafael. Growing up, he used to play barbies with me, and we would race hot wheel cars together. My favorite was riding our bikes down the red stairs from the house we lived in at Cullerton and 19th street in Pilsen, a neighborhood in Chicago. We had a blast climbing trees. Money was tight so we used to sleep on a mattress on the floor all together. Since my dad worked two shifts we did not see him much. I also remember me and my brother would whisper the night away hoping my dad would not hear us. Later, my second brother and the cutest chubby baby, Juan Razo, was born. I remember carrying him even if he was too heavy for my scrawny hands. Then, my only sister, Ruby Razo, came along. Finally, the baby of the family, Agustin, was born.

Out of all my siblings, I am the only immigrant and it truly was a scar in my life. Growing up, I faced many limitations. When I was in sixth grade, I wrote in my goal journal that I wanted to have a PhD in mathematics to help other Latinos like myself to learn and love math. Yes, at only twelve years old I had big crazy dreams. But being an immigrant was like a looming shadow that always followed me. In 2008, when the leaves from the trees began to turn different shades of color, my school counselor talked to my high school class about college. The counselor mentioned something called FAFSA, the government financial aid for U.S. citizens. Oh no! I knew I was not a U.S. Citizen. I started to get worried. In the back of my mind, I knew my parents said not to share my status out of fear of being deported and separated from our family. However, I still raised my hand and asked the counselor, "What if you are an immigrant?" With a hostile tone she said, "Well good luck. You can't get money. Plus, I don't even think it's legal for you to go to college in our country." The sound of these words was as if broken glass cut through my soft skin and pierced my dreams away. That was when I realized that the world was not such a happy place. The rejection and continuous "No," pressed on me until college.

I was not going to stop because the government was not going to financially help me. I researched the options for undocumented students going into higher education. Later, I created a presentation to educate others in my similar situation. I presented to hundreds of students at Curie High School and community organizations in Little Village. In addition, I made a scholarship fund for undocumented students called Students for Students Scholarship Fund. To this day, I continue to share my story, raising awareness and motivating others to get involved. I did not do this alone. I was supported by many on this journey.

MAKING MY OWN PATH

At eighteen, my life completely changed. I left my parents' house with my bags full of clothes and a box of notebooks from my high school math classes. I wrote a note stating that while I loved my parents, I was leaving to live with my boyfriend. I was afraid of my dad because he had always been very strict with me. So instead of facing him and asking him for permission to hang out with my boyfriend until curfew hours, I chose to leave. I drove away with the RAM 1500 my dad gifted me. I was heartbroken the first week. I wanted to go back because I missed my parents and especially my two-year-old baby brother, Agustin. I still remember giving him a kiss and telling him I was sorry for leaving him. Very dumb! I was just a freshman in college. While I do not advise any young person to leave their home that early in their life, I do not regret my choice. I learned to be independent and make my own path. I had endless college assignments plus I had to find a job to pay off a $12,000 annual tuition bill. I ended up working at Chipotle part time but it was not the right fit for me.

After I left my parents' home, my dad was very upset and gave me the silent treatment for about a year. But I had to let my pride go, so I finally reached out to him and asked if I could work for him. My father owns a pallet wood business, Guero's Pallets, Inc. He worked in a small warehouse he rented on 25th and Rockwell. He had me work after my class, sweeping the saw dust and cleaning the machines until I was able to cut wood using the table chop saw. It was very hard the first month. But I was not going to take a penny from my father. I wanted to earn my own money and pay for my college on my own. Soon, I realized I could not be working in the warehouse forever. I was getting a degree in mathematics, so I asked my dad if I could learn office work. He was running a company on his own and still had the shoe box approach for storing invoices and receipts. I was good with numbers but knew very little about business. So, I started looking into programs for bookkeeping. I found out about QuickBooks and learned it to the point that I became certified. I managed all the accounts receivable and payable using QuickBooks. I later took vendor accounts and started to manage the customer and vendor accounts. I learned all there was to do with pallets, pricing, machinery, and account managing.

We later started searching for our own warehouse space. It took three years for a bank to believe in us. I had to create reports and show the bank that we had no problems paying a mortgage for a 1 million+ property. My father and I were in disbelief when we were approved! In April 2016 we signed off on our pallet warehouse, a 2.75 acres property on 355 N. Lavergne Chicago, IL that we now own six years later in 2022. I no longer had to work inside of a semi-trailer as an office. I was more than excited and proud of my family's business achievement.

A few months later, I accepted an internship at Barclays as a data analyst in New York on Wall Street. I enjoyed working at Barclays. Sahana, my manager, was amazing. I worked on several projects. I built mathematical models to forecast sales revenue, I conducted assessments of various business intelligence tools and mobile solutions. I led demo sessions on data analytics and new technologies. I became an asset in such a short period that I taught my managers data analytics. I had my own sessions where I thought about topics such as modeling and forecasting. It was a wonderful experience where I learned and grew a lot. At the end of the internship, I was offered a full time position. However, I rejected the offer. I really missed my family and did not want to leave them for a second time.

I went back to Guero's Pellets and made it my mission to grow my family's company. I went to live with the love of my life Thomas Vazquez. Beautiful story, he was my mentor teacher when I met him. I chased him and conquered his heart. And now he cannot get rid of me because he cannot live without my silly self. Shortly after Barclays, I graduated from the Illinois Institute of Technology with a Bachelors and Master's degree in Applied Mathematics with a focus in statistics. I was eight months pregnant with my son, Angelo Vazquez, during my last semester at IIT and finishing my thesis. It was a challenging last semester, working and going to graduate school was a roller coaster. But I graduated!

That same year I created a one woman show showcasing my story of being undocumented titled, My Dream Fund, at

Loyola University. On July 27, 2017, I had my son and had to give the theater and my show a break. I left the project and put my doctorate degree on pause. It was not easy my first year as a mom. To expecting moms, please take all the maternity leave time and more. The one regret I have is that I only took 3 months of maternity leave and right after I put my son in daycare. I regret not spending more time in those early months with my little treasure. The baby stage is so short and yes, very difficult, but it just slips away so quickly. Do not miss the small moments for anything.

SUPERWOMAN

I took all I learned from IIT and my love for numbers, I used all data analytics and coding to drive Guero's Pallets forward. Even after the pandemic in 2019-2021 our business continued to grow. In 2021, our sales doubled, and our profit margins increased from 5% to 32%. Due to these astonishing accomplishments, I became CEO at Guero's Pallets at the end of 2021.

In my heart I was still missing my non-for-profit work helping elevate other undocumented students like myself. Along with my IIT colleagues, Karina Alcorchas and Cynthia, we started the 2% Fund, a non-profit whose mission is to increase the 2% of undocumented students in higher education via financing and mentorship.

My current project is my start-up, SOLIX, with Maryam Pishgar whom I met at UIC.

I was able to create growth at Guero's Pallets by using data driven decisions. SOLIX provides business data driven solutions to help companies grow. I can't wait to help millions of small companies succeed.

I am back in school at UIC in my second year pursuing a PhD in Industrial Engineering with a focus in process mining. In my first year, I published two papers in process mining in the medical field, "Process Mining Model to Predict Mortality in Paralytic Ileus Patients" and "Deep Learning Model for Mortality Prediction of ICU Patients with Paralytic Ileus". I am collaborating on a second paper that will be published in 2022 and creating my own algorithm for prediction of the next event.

Like my father when he was raising me, a lot of the time you do not know what you're doing, but as long as you have a goal, and keep making steps towards that goal, you do not give up. Even if you fall and look like a headless chicken doing it, you will make it further than you ever thought.

Just look at the story of my parents. They raised a successful young lady: a writer, a mathematician, an engineer, data analyst, an artist, and a badass businesswoman.

I want to do the same as my parents and pave the path for my son to reach greatness and happiness. And for the readers, let's make it happen. Set your goals so high they call you crazy!

REFLECTION QUESTIONS

1. What makes you happy, and why are you not doing more of it?

2. How can you spend more meaningful time with your loved ones?

3. What data can you collect to answer a key business question for your company's growth?

BIOGRAPHY

Martha Razo is a mathematician, pallet expert, salesperson, philanthropist, entrepreneur, writer, actress, and co-CEO and co-founder of Solix Services. She believes that with data-driven solutions a company can achieve real growth. Martha experiences the power of data in her own work at Guero's Pallets, Inc., where she oversees daily operations as CEO. Martha has a Bachelor's and a Master's from the Illinois Institute of Technology in Applied Mathematics. Martha is currently pursuing her PhD in Industrial Engineering at the University of Illinois at Chicago (UIC) with a focus on data and process mining.

Martha is the founder of the 2% Fund, a nonprofit whose mission is to increase undocumented students enrolled in higher education through financing and mentorship. In 2019, she co-authored My Dream Fund, a one-woman show about her story and how she overcame barriers as an immigrant to become the successful entrepreneur and educated, powerful woman she is today.

Martha has eight years of business experience and over six years experience analyzing big data and artificial intelligence. She brings tools for interpreting and analyzing business data and a strong foundation of what it takes to run a business. Her publications can be found on Google Scholar.

Martha Razo
(312) 523-5561
mrazo202@gmail.com
LinkedIn @Martha Razo

Dr. Alicia La Hoz

"Rejection is an invitation to dive into the past and, armed with jewels of truth, charge forward taking one wise step after another until you can sprint, run and fly."

I could barely sleep, anticipating the email that would apprise us of our future. At the crack of dawn, I opened my laptop and stared at the email for several minutes before I clicked to open it. I had to read it repeatedly to understand, *"I am sorry to inform you that you have not been matched."* The disappointment took hold, and as it shook me up inside, the pillars I had trusted came tumbling down. As I let the pain wash over me, my husband, Jose Arturo, held me trying to reassure me.

For eleven years, I prepared for this day. I questioned the years of discipline, sacrifice, time, and financial resources invested in pursuing higher education. *"Was it all worth it?"* It seemed that no matter how hard I tried, how much effort I put in, how much-focused ambition I orchestrated—the door was going to close shut, and I was going to be left out.

The last year of the doctoral degree in psychology involves a full-time internship. Before this internship, you are placed in yearly practicums—a type of part-time unpaid internship where you work with diverse clinical settings under the supervision of a Licensed Clinical Psychologist. It's free labor, and often you have a less than optimal experience completing tasks no one else wants to do. I was blessed and had many enriching experiences including clinicians watching through a mirror as I conducted counseling sessions and giving me on-demand feedback by interrupting the session to suggest interventions. I conducted psychological testing for behavioral health as treatment recommendations for clinicians and even for forensic purposes to inform the judicial system. I did play therapy with children and adolescents in the foster care system coordinating treatment with social workers, guardian ad litem, and parents.

The final full-time internship of the doctoral program involves a rigorous interview process. I had spent months applying and preparing for interviews. I was possessed by the idea that I could become a Psychologist in the Air Force. After passing what I thought was a rigorous physical test, I was invited to interview with several Air Force bases around the nation. I also applied to many community clinics. Our finances were stretched to the brim as I crisscrossed the country. I enthusiastically shared with my husband everything about the city, about how the interview went, and about the possibilities that lay ahead.

After preparing and investing so much for so long, students wait with angst for what can be a magical morning or a devastating one. Most students are offered employment where they intern. In a way, the email is revered like a crystal ball prophesying your future. Students rank the locations they would like to be placed in order of preference. Sites interviewed do the same, and the system "matches" these. Then, one fateful morning, everyone involved receives an email notifying both agencies and students where they will be headed.

After I shed many tears following match day, I took cautious steps as I walked down the corridor to the student room separated for the doctoral students in our program. I felt my ears burn as I heard the whispers among classmates about the number of students that did not match that year. I cringed as I tried to sort out my options and what to do next. I fought the shame burbling to the surface when I met the sympathy in my friend's eyes. *"What was wrong with me?"* I thought while I shrugged it off and calmly said, *"It will be okay,"* more for my benefit than theirs. While I smiled widely for those, who had successfully landed in places they wanted to go to and accepted my lot, I fought the thoughts of insecurity that crouched in the corners of my heart, *"Why was I not good enough?"* The training and my faith helped me not let these thoughts nest in my heart. Still, it was a moment-by-moment battle to shoo them away as I wondered where they originated.

FACING REJECTION REVEALS THE ORIGINS OF SHAME

A picture came to mind as I struggled to make sense of my reality and the shaky ground I stood on. While a freshman in high school, I remembered sitting in a classroom frustrated. I loved to learn, and because of testing standards, I ended up in these general education classes in an overcrowded school in South Florida. I had fought hard during my elementary and middle school years to graduate from the English as A Second Language (ESL) and remedial classes I had been placed in.

When I was eight years old, I came to the U.S. but prior to that, I attended a private education in the Dominican Republic, where I was born and raised. My mother had founded two private schools in the country. My younger sister and I would sing a little tune, "A mi me gusta la escuela de allá, a mi no me gusta la escuela de aquí, (I like school from over there, I don't like school here) making sure everyone knew loud and clear that we were miserable. The only class I liked was math because it was the only one I understood. While it didn't take too long to learn to speak English, I was behind on everything else: reading comprehension, history, and science, thereby doing poorly in standardized testing. Despite my desire and best intentions to learn, I was stuck in classrooms that were a joke.

Disappointing classroom experiences flooded my mind. In the fourth grade, I faithfully sat in the back because there were many National Geographic magazines that I could read while ignoring the unruly class. So here I was in high school, and the nightmare of fourth grade repeating itself. *Wasn't this high school? Wasn't I out of the remedial classes? Why wasn't this any better?"* Time moved slow as sloth, and I recollected how my anger bubbled up inside of me into a controlled rage. This time, the teacher wasn't the object being ridiculed—he joined in the fun mocking students. As I counted the minutes to be released, I decided. I said to myself, *"I am going to get out of here; I am going to do whatever I can to get ahead; I am going to fight for me."* The system would not dictate who I was and who I would be. I drew strength at home where I found refuge in my father's steady presence and unwavering faith, the energetic zeal and compassion of my mom, and in the focused perseverance of my five sisters.

As I remembered my past, I finally let myself be angry. I was angry at systems that required me to keep finding ways to jump over or run around in circles to get to the other side. When I felt miserable in mindless jobs to make ends meet, I would give myself a pep talk, *"This is only the means to an end. It is a season, and this too will pass. Just hold on."* I held on to the vision for my dear life so I could put up with the discomforts. In a way, I felt betrayed by education. It was supposed to have my back. Now, what did I have to show for my faithfulness?

What was I supposed to do? Without an internship, you couldn't graduate. Without an internship, you couldn't get the needed hours required for licensure, which meant you couldn't work in the field. And the pile of graduate student loans incurred would come knocking down the door soon. How was I supposed to pay?

FACING THE ANGER AND CORRECTING ASSUMPTIONS

I had a reckoning with God. I honestly laid out my frustration and anger, and he met me. I felt his peace and comfort grip me. The rage and the doubts it festered lifted. The expectations I had created throughout the year of investigating and interviewing for internships, the academic pressure I had put on myself - it all evaporated.

I later learned that from 2000-2006 (the years I participated in the match), 18% of the students who applied in this process did not match. I didn't know that the number of applicants had exceedingly surpassed the number of internship slots available until I had a chance to talk to my advisor. He reassured me that a clearinghouse would open, and that not all was lost. He encouraged me to stay positive and promised to help. I went back to the computer room to learn about the clearinghouse with my head held high. A few hours later, my advisor called me, *"I have an interview set up for you for tomorrow."*

The relief and gratitude that burst in my heart is hard for me to explain, *"Would I dare to hope again?"* With rekindled optimism, I put on my best self and headed to the interview meeting the Clinical Director of Meier Clinics, Dr. Brad Kahle. I vividly recall the encounter. We both talked about how the interview was providential and that we knew that God wanted me there.

Eighteen years later, I now run a nationally recognized not-for-profit organization, Family Bridges, founded during my internship year at Meier Clinics. Family Bridges seeks to end the cycle of family trauma through innovative programs that empower, equip, and encourage underserved communities. Out of the 230 awarded healthy marriage and family federal guarantees since 2006, Family Bridges was the only Latina-led organization out of 8 awarded in three funding cycles for $30 Million. In addition, we outsourced over $14 Mil in shared services to local community agencies, effectively delivering prevention programs in over 700 partnering agencies. These included women's correctional facilities, hospitals, substance abuse centers, shelters, churches, community centers, and other civic and public centers effectively reaching minority groups.

REJECTION IS FUEL FOR GROWTH

It all started with a rejection. Fear of rejection can keep you frozen in time. You can stay paralyzed behind its power, or you can stand up and take the next wise step, the next wise step, and then the next wise step. Then, you sprint, run, and one day you fly.

Advocating for resources for the least of these, for those in the margin, for those in painful relational situations, has meant that I have had to deal with a significant share of rejection. Each time the pain lessens, and I am quicker to bounce back up. In retrospect, some of the dreams I pushed for might have been outsized for the time or diverted our path. I've learned how to carry through the hardship with a spirit of contentment and how to dial into the support of my family and friends. I've learned to lean in my faith in Christ and through prayer I have healed, changed perspective, and found the strength to stay on course.

You can choose to stay frozen, reading one page of the book over and over again, contemplating the Whys of the rejection. Or you can turn the page and see the plot unfold.

Don't you owe it to yourself to see the rest of the story? Don't miss out on the climax and unexpected ending. Keep knocking on doors—and often, the doors you least expect will open to unbelievable experiences, opportunities, and growth. When the doors are shut, your grit, endurance, confidence, and resilience will grow, and along the way, you will show others how life is best lived.

REFLECTION QUESTIONS

1. In your own experience of rejection, what vulnerabilities did it reveal? What did you feel?

2. How has this rejection shaped you into who you are today?

3. What do you need to be bold and take the next wise step forward?

BIOGRAPHY

For 22 years, Dr. Alicia La Hoz has brought psychological and social science research-based principles on mental health, leadership, professional development and family life with a community-based approach.

She obtained a Doctorate in Psychology from Wheaton College in 2004 and a Masters in Counseling Psychology from Trinity International University in 2001. She founded Family Bridges, a family strengthening not-for-profit organization operating in Chicago, Phoenix, Portland with affiliates in several Latin American cities. Dr. La Hoz also expanded her imprint globally through a mini-drama series, ¡Qué Gente, Mi Gente!, airing in 26 radio markets worldwide.

She has developed research-based curricula on conflict-resolution and stress management with a trauma-informed approach based on outcomes of programs delivered to more than 165,000 persons. She has delivered professional development to key leaders and staff in a diversity of organizations including fortune 500 companies leading to the formation of BridgesXL focused on coaching and leadership development.

In 2013, Dr. La Hoz authored the toolkit for *Stakeholders Working with Latino Individuals, Couples and Families* published by the National Resource Center for Healthy Marriage and Families and Romance Perpetuo, a resource workbook for Latino couples. In 2017, she co-authored the *Struggle Is Real: Modern Parenting*, a book and multi-media podcast.

For four years Dr. La Hoz served on the Hispanic Research Work Group held by the Office of Planning, Research, and Evaluation within the Administration of Children and Families, U.S., HHS. Currently, she serves in the Family Life Board, a ministry of CRU.

Dr. Alicia La Hoz
alicia@familybridgesusa.org
LinkedIn: /alicia-la-hoz-pysd

BE ROOTED. GROW DEEP. STAND TALL.

Nancy C. Vasser

"A tree is never planted in the wrong place."

It was August 2019, and I was enjoying my maternity leave during the warm summer. My second son, Jordan, was born in July and we would often take walks around the neighborhood. The streets were lined with trees showcasing several shades of green. During one of my many walks, my husband called to inform me that water had flooded my in-laws' basement. A sewer pipe was backed-up from tree roots that made their way into the pipes. It would cost thousands of dollars to clean out. I began to ponder about the forgotten life system that grows under my feet. Nature's intricate underground plumbing providing support to the beautiful trees standing in front of me. The strength and persistence of tree roots are a force to be reckoned with. Mother Nature consistently challenges trees with high winds, lightning, storms, and droughts. I thought about how these same roots adapted to their surroundings and grew through anything in their way. I began to envision my roots, my tree, the growth, and challenges that have grounded me. I took inventory of all the people around me throughout my life and realized that each mentor, challenge, and opportunity helped me dig my roots deeper. Each lesson helped stabilize me. I prevailed but the failures were equally as important in contributing to the strength and persistence. I realized then that God surrounds us with many ways to learn and hear from Him. It was time to take note.

TAPROOTS

My diverse root system began to develop years ago in Central and North America. My parents immigrated to the United States in the 1970s from Mexico (Father) and Nicaragua (Mother) escaping extreme poverty. Each of them overcoming serious hardships–early loss of a parent, hunger, poverty, and violence. I admired their strength and persistence. They left their families, culture, and language to courageously pursue a better life in a foreign land. There was no immigrant starter kit, financial assistance, social media, or manual to follow. My parents settled humbly in Chicago with their three daughters (Erica, Diana, Nancy). At the surface level the growth was not visible but deep down their perseverance was paying off. Their strength and love would nourish three growing seedlings.

My mother would tell you blatantly that I was unplanned–my two older sisters kept my parents busy and there was no plan for a third child. Upon finding out that she was pregnant with me my mom presented my father with two options: 1) an abortion for $300 or 2) we keep the baby. My father decided to keep me. Like the pregnancy, my birth was also unexpected. I was born premature via emergency c-section on a very cold Thanksgiving Day. I do have an attitude of gratitude and love food so it was only appropriate. Dad named me after his favorite fruit in Mexico – Nance (yellow cherry). The "e" was replaced with a "y" due to the language barrier.

Growing up in a typical Chicago neighborhood like Humboldt Park in the 90's meant fire hydrant splash parties, walking to the corner store for $0.25 chips and ice cream, and playing outside until the street lights came on. We had to look out for gangs as we made our walks to and from school every day. We also needed to worry about the threat of potential pyromaniacs looming in our neighborhood. My cousin lived a few houses south across the street from us. One morning, I was startled awake by a frantic pounding on the front door—it was my cousin Michelle. "My house is on fire!" she sobbed. Sadly, this same scenario would happen to my cousin's family again after they attempted to rebuild. Several other houses on our block would also suffer the same fate. On a separate occasion I remember coming home and our house had been broken into. I remember my sister crying uncontrollably and my father yelling at her to stop. In the coming weeks my father added metal bars to our windows. The smell of smoke and sirens would haunt me for years. My parents decided to leave Chicago for the western suburbs in hopes of changing the course for our family roots.

PERMANENT DIVERSE ROOTS

I was sad to move. I did not want to leave my friends or neighborhood—it was all that I knew. Despite being nervous about starting over, I quickly acclimated to suburbia life. My new friends helped me to quickly forget my old neighborhood. The street light curfew was still in effect and I managed to extend it a bit in our safer neighborhood. I also became more independent in my new dwelling. My father worked the 1st shift and my mother worked the 2nd shift so I needed to do things for myself like getting ready for school and taking the bus. I also managed my schoolwork on my own with little to no intervention from my parents. I spent a lot of time with my father fixing cars, gardening, swimming, and riding my bike. The weekends were for grocery shopping, family parties, and watching The Three Stooges.

One day in 8th grade, I was sitting in music class fiddling with the keyboard. The music teacher would go around the room and ask each student what they wanted to go to college for. It was my turn and I proudly said, "I don't want to go to college!" I could see the disappointment in the teacher's face. I forget her response but she tried to talk me out of it. My answer was not uncommon amongst the group. At least ninety five percent of the classroom did not have a parent/guardian who graduated college and it was not a goal that we worked towards. The concept was foreign. In fact I can't remember looking up to anyone within our family or friends that went to college. In my household getting a high school diploma was the goal and highest accomplishment.

EMBRACE THE STORM

My parents sent me to a private Catholic high school in hopes that I would be exposed to a better crowd. My high school experience really did expose me to another "world". A world of families with better resources, money, higher education, and limited diversity. Witnessing this made me imagine and dream for bigger things. I too could educate myself, have a career, and provide for my family. I also wanted to be a role model to my niece. Every month, I would stop by the main office to make tuition payments and I was reminded of what our family did not have. My parents made tuition payments paycheck to paycheck. I believe at least eighty percent or more of our graduating class had been accepted into college and I was one of them. I loved my parents' proud smiles after I received my high school diploma. My mother snatched that diploma out of my hands before I could give her a hug and said, *"Esto es mio"* (this is mine). It was time to raise the bar for our family.

It was my junior year of college when my father sat me down in our living room. He sheepishly said, "I lost my job, and I can't help you pay for school anymore. You can quit school and get a job" I did not flinch, but quitting was not an option. I thought of Cortes and his expedition to the Americas–let all the ships burn, I am not turning back. I needed to adapt. At the time, I worked as a bank teller and marched into the branch the next day "I need more hours!" I told my branch manager. I remember sitting alone in the corner of the teller line having an anxiety attack before the branch closed that evening. I thought, "How the hell am I going to do this?" The following semesters I would try to take classes two days a week and work the rest. I also would work an eight hour day then take a night class afterwards. I was working close to forty hour weeks with a full-time school load and busy social life.

My senior year of college I just wanted to hurry up and be done. I desperately wanted my big girl job with a big girl salary. My family helped with housing, supplies, and books but I needed to fund all other aspects of my life. I signed myself up for a hefty class schedule to get ahead and needed counselor approval to proceed. My counselor looked at me and said, "I don't think you can handle all of these classes." I sat there in disbelief–why the hell not? I couldn't relate to their perception of the college experience–I did not have unlimited financial support–I was barely trying to stay afloat.

I disputed his opinion, made my case, and he hesitated but he did eventually sign off on my request. When graduation came around my counselor commended me "I didn't think you were going to do it but you did". It was validating to prove to him that I could dig deep and stay focused. On graduation day my mother once again proudly snatched the diploma out of my hands and said, *"Esto es mío también"*. Time to raise the bar again.

MY GROWTH, MY RESPONSIBILITY

I stumbled upon my banking career years ago mostly looking for flexibility while in school. Over the course of my eighteen year banking career the industry taught me to learn about money management. I learned how to navigate concepts and plan for the future. My parents were also learning how to navigate their finances. My father was a true saver, no credit cards, pay in cash kind of a guy which defined their value of a dollar. I believe that if my family knew how to better manage their money we would have accumulated more wealth. It took many years to untangle myself from their negative beliefs on money. I understand now their beliefs were a product of their poverty and I can reject the parts that do not serve my growth. Going forward I can honor their sacrifices by helping build generational wealth for our family. As I look back and reflect on my life I want to be the change in the world I did not experience. While I did have a solid support system of friends and family—I would have liked to have shared in more experiences with successful Latinos.

From nature's perspective a tree is never planted in the wrong place. The tree spends years growing its intricate roots and understands there is strength in time. Roots expand below the surface before their essence takes on the world above. This hard work is often overlooked as it can't be seen. My roots began with my parents' courage to uproot and begin a life on unknown soil. What you see before you are the fruits of their labor, love, support, and sacrifice. I took on the easy part—born in a country of opportunity, freedoms, and making the most of it. Carl Jung said, "No tree, it is said, can grow to heaven unless its roots reach down to hell." The rejections, the lack of money, the extra hours, the tears, the anxiety, and nightmares made me grow and dig deeper. I now proudly own our stories, the sacrifices, and challenges. I remind myself to never forget my roots.

REFLECTION QUESTIONS

1. Who helped plant your tap roots and how have they shaped your success?

2. Reflect on the storms. How did they make you dig deep? Reference this when another storm is brewing.

3. How do you connect with nature around you? We often enjoy nature's beauty but consider all that goes into sustaining it.

BIOGRAPHY

Nancy C. Vasser has worked in the banking industry for over 18 years and is currently a Senior Vice President at Wintrust Private Client. She leads a team that provides service and support to sales, investment, and credit professionals. Nancy holds a B.S. in Business Administration from Elmhurst College.

Nancy is passionate about lifting others up. She serves on the board for Love Purse. Love Purse collects purses filled with toiletries and donates the items to women experiencing domestic abuse, homelessness, and other trials. Each Love Purse contains a personal, handwritten note to encourage recipients of their worth. Nancy also serves on the board for the International Women of Influence who empowers women by creating a platform for them to share their stories. They also promote networking, businesses, and involvement within local communities.

In her spare time Nancy is plotting her next expedition. Her wanderlust has led her to visit many different parts of the world but there are more adventures to be made and stories to tell. She enjoys visiting one of her favorite mentors – the ocean. The ocean reminds her not to get tied down by the challenges and make waves of her own. Nancy lives in the Midwest with her husband and two sons. The snowy cold gloomy winters remind her that water is best kept at room temperature.

Nancy C. Vasser
vassernancy@gmail.com

Natalia C. Franco

"For now we see only a reflection[c] as in a mirror, but then face to face. Now I know in part, but then I will know fully, as I am fully known. 13 Now these three remain: faith, hope, and love—but the greatest of these is love." 1 Cor 13:12-13 CSB

This story is about the greatest love I've known. While I wish it was like a fairy tale or Hollywood movie, it involves lots of tears, despair, and sorrow. Nonetheless it is a story of life and rebirth. It is a story of how I lost it all for love, or so I thought. People say that no one dies of heartache, but that is not my experience. The pain I felt did kill a part of me, a part that needed to die so the real me could come out. This story is about how I found myself in the middle of so much chaos and became a living testimony that love always wins!

WHAT DOESN'T KILL YOU MAKES YOU STRONGER

In pursuit of that perfect love, I ended up in many toxic relationships, including two failed marriages. My last divorce was my breaking point. It woke me up and made me stop and search for my truth. It made me question my decisions and go beyond my fears, to no longer blame others, and start looking for answers within me. While at times I still struggle to accept my fate, I am forever grateful for the pain that led me to this path of self-discovery. It isn't easy to talk about what hurts us, yet it is very rewarding because we not only free ourselves, but we open the door for others to do the same. It takes courage, humility, and some confidence to own our story.

DYING TO RISE

I am from Colombia. I went back when my son was four years old, and I was trying to put space between my ex and I after my first divorce. There I could provide my son things I couldn't afford in the States: a nanny, private education, a chance to learn Spanish, and our culture.

While in Colombia, I met a man at work. Unfortunately, he was married when we started dating (something I deeply regret to this day). My lover not only struggled with some truths about his life, but also suffered from addiction, alcohol, which led to other emotional issues.

Our relationship was chaotic from the beginning. In my own blindness the more I stayed the more I fell in love with him and the more I ignored every red flag. He became my everything, my life, my all. I became addicted to him. In psychological terms they call this codependency: an excessive emotional or psychological reliance on a partner, typically one who requires support on account of an illness or addiction. In my case he became the center of my universe.

After three painful years with this man, I decided to

return home with my son. My devotion to my lover led me to ask him to come along. During one of his visits, he proposed to me (I accepted) and we headed to the States to begin a new life together. Our marriage was beyond challenging, we fought so much. It was very toxic; we went from love to hate within minutes and the abuse just increased. In the beginning, I was more silent and grew fearful of his anger. I would apologize to avoid ruining the moment, felt guilty, and would try not to do things that bothered him. As time passed, I too became verbally aggressive and even acted in harmful ways. Sometimes I felt like I was an alcoholic myself without even taking a drink. That is what alcoholism does, it infects not only the one who suffers it but those who surround them. At times I would leave to avoid fighting and sleep somewhere else: my car, my best friend's house, our own couch, or hotels. My body started to give up on me and I ended up fighting precancerous cells in my uterus. Despite it all I would always come back to him. After his hangover was gone, we would hug, kiss and make up. Things worsened between us and his struggles so much so that he hit rock bottom and ended up in rehab getting help. I was left broken, scared, and without a clue as to where our marriage would land.

I wish I could say that was the end of my misery and I moved on, but that was not the case. The day he called, as usual, I went back to him. We tried to stay together for one more year. This time he was sober, so I figured our problems were solved, we were left without excuses to become a healthy couple and build a family. Unfortunately, we had nothing to save anymore and no matter how much we denied ourselves, the truth was right in front us. After eight long years of struggle, so many tears, heart aches, and total exhaustion trying to save a broken marriage, in March of 2020 my husband did what I never could: he finally left. I was devastated, heartbroken, my chest physically hurt to even breath and all I saw was a dark empty hole.

YOU WILL KNOW THE TRUTH AND THE TRUTH SHALL SET YOU FREE

In the field of addiction, it is believed that the addict needs to hit rock bottom before he/she is willing to admit their condition and begin recovery. Looking back, I think that is exactly what happened to me. That marriage was my total bottom. It got me to my darkest place but from there, there was nowhere else to go but towards the light. And light I became!

A month into my grieving I decided to seek help. I needed to crawl out from that hole, to save myself, if not for me but for my son. By then I had been attending CODA (Codependent Anonymous) and other 12-step programs. I was diagnosed with PTSD (Post Traumatic Stress Disorder), severe anxiety, severe depression, and my self-esteem was below normal, a failing two out of ten. My therapist and I started to work with EMDR, a therapy that has proven to be very effective to treat trauma and other treatments too.

Therapy led me to find answers and the true source of my pain. Of course, it had nothing to do with my ex. What was the true source of my pain? A very aching childhood, so hurtful to me that my brain had decided to block the pain completely. I come from a family who suffers from the same condition as my ex-husband. Despite their good intentions, my parents were mostly absent struggling with their own issues and addictions. They were unable to nurture me and provide a healthy environment where I could feel accepted, validated, safe, and loved. Instead of hallmark childhood memories I got stuck in a circle of emotional, psychological, and at times physical abuse. I lost my own sense of self, totally afraid of life. I became a survivor and in the process a rescuer too which I portrayed through romantic relationships. In a subconscious way, I was just trying to rescue my parents.

THE ONLY WAY OUT IS THROUGH

It is said that the only way out is through, and that is what therapy did for me. It created a safe environment in which I could go through all the grief I held back. Little by little I started feeling the pain and mourned the loss of my childhood, my innocence, and my adolescence. It wasn't easy, and at times still isn't, but it is necessary. It's the only way to make room for my true self and new emotions. My new therapist says, "To remember is not to relive things". This keeps me grounded.

If we want to live free, we need to unpack our feelings, to step into our darkness. To embrace our scars and not let the pain of our past define us. Like the fire that burns the charcoal to let the diamond come out and shine, if we allow it, feelings will burn the pain that holds us back until the only thing left is the diamond within us.

RECOVERY IS A JOURNEY NOT A DESTINATION

Along the way I've realized that I am not alone in my experience. So many people have gone through similar struggles as mine. My pain connects me deeper and stronger to others. I've connected to so many people, especially women, who have suffered in so many ways. Some of them are part of my support group and my go-to people when I need guidance, or simply a friend to talk to. No one makes it alone and realizing it has been very valuable to my recovery. We all need allies, a support group, and people that speak our language to guide us.

Learning to love myself has become my journey. From finding the courage to see me, to accepting me, to finding forgiveness for myself. I prayed for the ability to love myself the way I loved others and with little steps every day, I've learned to accept myself as I am, to embrace my pain and in doing so I found this amazing love for myself.

AND ~~THEY~~ SHE LIVES HAPPILY EVER AFTER...

To love others, we must love ourselves first. This journey of true love, to finding my real dreams, helped me find my purpose in life. Today I know that all that happened to me was my destiny so I could help other beautiful women that still suffer in those dark places I was once in.

I found my journey to be more magical than the Disney love stories. It does include princesses and princes but not necessarily finding a happy ending together. Instead, I found a beautiful princess in me worthy of all the love I was born with and the true deserving person of it all. The more I love myself, the more life shines upon me. The more passion I find in pursuing my dreams, the more alive I feel, and the more I find reasons to smile.

This is my story. The story of how loving an addict led me to finding my true love. The story of a woman whose love saved her and brought her to life. The story of how in the middle of the chaos I found that great love we all dream of, that love that makes us whole...I found myself!

REFLECTION QUESTIONS

1. Have you ever hit rock bottom? What did it look like for you to come out from the lowest point in your life?

2. What is the true source of your pain? Ask a professional for help to dig deep and face any pain that is stopping you from growing.

3. Who or what are you living for?

BIOGRAPHY

Natalia Carvajal Franco is a proud Latina passionate about helping women struggling with emotional and mental health. Through her own personal journey, she has found a new purpose and looks forward to becoming a mental health counselor to assist executives struggling with abuse. She graduated with a bachelor's degree in Information Technology with a minor in marketing while going through a divorce, bankruptcy and being a new mom. During her second marriage and relocation to the States she joined a fortune 500 company working as a Senior Manager in the technology area.

In 2020, she graduated with her MBA with honors and became the first woman in her family with a master's degree. She served as the President of the BIBA (Business Intelligence, Business Analytics Association) Student organization and was invited to become part of the President's Elite Club at her university. She has always been an advocate for helping others and established a mindfulness program to support her colleagues' mental health. Today, she is committed to supporting the Latino community by creating alliances to help Latinos who struggle with addictions and other emotional related dependencies on their journey towards recovery. Natalia looks forward to completing her second master's degree in clinical mental health counseling.

Natalia C. Franco
nat@nataliacfranco.com
Instagram: @natisc83
LinkedIn:/nataliacarvajalf
954-404-3382

Lorena Martínez

"Cada Uno Cosecha Lo Que Siembra."
You reap what you sow.

Being successful and feeling successful can be two completely different places. As a first-generation Mexican woman, I have heard many people tell me that I am very successful and that at thirty-six years old, it's wonderful to see everything I have accomplished. Surprisingly, I have only felt successful the last couple of years of my life as an entrepreneur. Becoming aware of the beliefs and emotions that were not allowing me to honor my gifts and accomplishments has been life changing. I found myself trying to balance my crazy life as an individual, wife, mom, and leader. In the last two years, I realized that I had been in a constant modern dilemma that many Latinas face in honoring our heritage and traditions while building a new life with careers and lifestyles that are very different from what our parents provided us. I realized that for me to build the life I dreamed of, I needed to release feelings of guilt, self-sacrifice, limiting beliefs around money, and unworthiness.

The process of self discovery often brought me back to one of my favorite phrases that my father shared with me, "Cada uno cosecha lo que siembra" (you reap what you sow). Transforming old beliefs has been a process because it required me to go through a cycle that involves awareness, acceptance, and action. I had to become aware of the emotions, accept them, and do something about it to change it. This process has been transformative because I now take complete ownership of my life choices. Healing parts of my childhood trauma has cleared old wounds and created room for new life experiences. Acknowledging feelings and becoming aware of my self-sabotaging coping mechanisms like perfectionism, people pleasing, imposter syndrome, and unworthiness has opened an internal dialogue with myself to become aware, accept, and transform my old belief systems. Allowing myself to accept my gifts and become the best version of myself has now become my priority. For the first time in my life, I made myself a priority and have made a commitment to taking care of myself first. My healing journey has allowed me to reflect on my life and become a witness of my past, present, and even my future. The story of my life I share today is through my perspective and is also through my father's shared wisdom.

PLANTANDO SEMILLAS. PLANTING SEEDS.

Reflecting on my childhood and healing these parts opened new doors for success. I realized that the seeds that my father and my family planted in me were the values that have been carried from generation to generation. At the same time, I know there were also some seeds that were planted in me that I no longer chose to nourish. Healing trauma was not often talked about in my family or in our Mexican culture and it has a huge impact on our success. My external world was a reflection of my internal mindset.

My mom died at thirty-one years old leaving behind my dad, my older sister, and I. This event changed my life forever and was the root case of some of my low self-esteem and negative self-worth. In a way I thought that if I wasn't worthy of having a mom, I wasn't worthy of having many other things such as joy and happiness. Since I was so little, I couldn't process this trauma and my family was not equipped with the awareness or tools to know I probably needed therapy because they themselves were also dealing with their own generational trauma.

My dad was a seasonal migrant farm worker and would go to Watsonville, California to work in the fields for the season. Moving to a new country from rural Mexico was a whole experience in itself. I was twelve, going through puberty, in middle school, and didn't know any English. Sounds like fun, right? Not! Little did I know that this was going to be the stepping-stone for the rest of my life. The values that were instilled in me early on such as dedication, work ethic, and resilience by my dad, my grandma, and my family in Mexico were the tools that helped me survive the move and excel in school.

CULTIVANDO. CULTIVATING

My experience as a first generation immigrant seemed very similar to many other children of immigrants from Mexico. I felt I had to do well in school so I could go to college, have a good job, and someday be able to repay my father for all the sacrifices he made when we came to the United States. I never thought my story or experiences were anything special. In a way, I thought I needed to do everything right so I didn't disappoint my family and, as a result, I started to put a lot of self-inflicted pressure to always perform. Internally, I would compare myself to my dad and think that my struggles were nothing compared to his struggles.

I got accepted to public and private colleges and decided to attend Sacramento State in the fall of 2003. The fact that I had met my now husband and he also was attending Sacramento State may or may not have affected my decision but that is another story. I moved out, worked part time and was financially independent. I took it upon myself to apply to all the scholarships and financial aid I could to ease the financial stress for my dad of going to college. My efforts literally paid off and I was able to graduate debt free from college. I received financial and moral support from the College Assistance Migrant Program and Early Opportunity Program at Sacramento State. In four years, I had my degree in Business Administration-Accountancy. I was also part of Inroads, a program whose mission was to place talented minorities in the fortune five hundred corporate American companies. Inroads was the bridge that placed me with PricewaterhouseCoopers, one of the big four public accounting firms.

I attribute my college and corporate experiences to cultivating the environment that allowed me to grow from a seed into the entrepreneur and leader I am now. I now look back and acknowledge that I did a great job surviving college given the fact that half of the time I didn't know what I was doing. If it wasn't for the support and guidance of the college programs, I would have been very lost. The hard work that I put in throughout college and also navigating corporate America gave me perspective and life experiences that I apply in my life as a business owner and leader.

During the 2008 recession, I had a quarter life crisis and ended up quitting my corporate job in Silicon Valley to pursue my passion and become a hairstylist. It was in big part due to corporate burnout. For the first time in my life, I was getting symptoms of corporate burnout and the life I had worked hard to build was crumbling in front of my eyes. I felt guilty for wanting to do something else because I grew up always caring about what people say about me. I felt so much internal pressure from working so hard to be where many people aspired to be. The "I should be grateful I have a good job" part kept me from recognizing that I wasn't fulfilled at my job. During this time, I felt as if all my family's dreams, hopes, and sacrifices rested on my shoulders. I was going to be a failure if I decided to walk away from the American Dream. Even though I was twenty-five, married, and felt like an adult, I dreaded telling my dad I was quitting my job to be a hairstylist. Little did I know that he would be so supportive and become one of my number one mentors. I will never forget his words when I told him: "Tu sabes lo que te conviene mejor a ti mija" (you know what is best for you). I quit my job in January 2010 and enrolled in cosmetology school. In October of that same year I co-founded The Colour Bar Salon with my husband.

LA COSECHA. HARVEST

My father's wise words have accompanied me throughout my life. Our conversations have always been about showing me that I will receive what I give, that if I am not getting the results I want, I need to change my actions.

I know I don't need to go into detail about what happened to the entire world in 2020. This was the first time in my life that I was forced to face everything I had harvested in the past, was currently harvesting, and the current seeds I was planning to harvest soon. In the six months that The Colour Bar salon was shut down because of the pandemic, I was able to reflect on my career as a business owner. Witnessing actions, patterns, and decisions, from an outside perspective and not in the day-to-day operations allowed me to face what was helping me and not helping me become the leader I aspire to be.

In those six months, I also focused on my personal development like never before in my life. I focused a lot of this time on healing my childhood trauma through energy healing therapy. I listened to a lot of audiobooks ranging from self-help, leadership, and psychology as well as invested in personal coaching. I had conversations with my dad that I did not have the courage to before. I will forever cherish his response the day I asked him if he was proud of me. Looking at me with love and respect he said, "Mija, I am more than proud of you". I was able to connect the dots looking back at all the seeds I had planted with my conditioning, coping mechanisms, and it was clear how personal growth, healing, and personal development affected my ability to benefit or limit my success.

I reflected on the life that my husband and I built with our two sons and two hair salon locations. He also quit his corporate job as a software engineer to become a full time officer at our company. As crazy as it might sound, I still didn't feel successful even with all of our accomplishments. I didn't fully recognize that success, happiness, and feeling accomplished can come in many forms. I now recognize that my life experiences have led me to be who I am as an individual, a mother, a wife, and a leader. If I took any of those experiences out, I wouldn't be me.

In the same way that I no longer let my past traumas define me, I also don't let my awards or success define me. My worth is no longer defined by how much I can achieve, how perfect I can be, or how much money I make. I now value myself for who I am. My awareness has also allowed me to gain perspective and realize that we are all in this world dealing with internal battles. I know many Latinas are also facing very similar challenges. Many times, I have faced challenges when trying to achieve harmony between all the different parts of me. I finally accepted that I can't be all of them at the same time. Some days feel accomplished in all areas and other days I feel I can't get anything right. I now focus more on being present. I also strive to carry my father's values and wisdom through my sons so that one day they learn how to plant their seeds, cultivate their environment, and harvest their own future the way they dream it to be.

REFLECTION QUESTIONS

1. As a Latina, what family values have helped you become successful?

2. How can you correlate your personal story to your professional success?

3. Could you relate to any of my personal struggles or challenges as a professional Latina?

BIOGRAPHY

Lorena Martinez is a proud native of Michoacán, Mexico. She came to Watsonville, California at the age of 12 and lived there with her family until she moved to Sacramento to attend college. Lorena obtained a degree of Business Administration–Accountancy from California State University, Sacramento. After working a few years in Silicon Valley at one of the big four public accounting firms, PircewaterhouseCoopers, she decided to make a career and life changing move towards working on her true passion as a hairstylist.

Lorena Martinez is a co-founder of The Colour Bar Salon, one of Sacramento's fastest growing and highly rated hair salons. She has taken the company from a single chair salon suite to one of the top rated salons in Sacramento, California. Since its founding in 2010, The Colour Bar has been rated "Best Place to Get Your Hair Done" for five consecutive years (2015-2019), "Best Place to Get Pampered" in 2019 by Sacramento News & Review and "Best Place to Work" in 2021 by the Sacramento Business Journal.

In 2021, she also co-founded Love Your Hair, an ecommerce website dedicated to providing high quality products. Lorena has been the recipient of three distinguished business awards: 2018 Hispanic Chamber of Commerce Latina Rising Estrella Award, 2019 Sacramento Business Journal Women Who Mean Business Award and 2019 Sacramento Business Journal 40 Under 40 award. Lorena is a strong believer and supporter of following your passion and doing what you love.

Lorena Martinez
Email: lorena@thecolourbar.me
IG: lorena_thecolourbar
FG: TheColourBar

LIBERATION

❧

Erica Priscilla Sandoval, LCSW

"Success is not about how much money you make. It's about how much you love yourself enough to heal."

ACCEPTANCE

I owe my life to my abuelito. When I was only a year old, my abuelito lost his life saving mine during a horrific car accident. In his absence, my abuelita became a young widow with six children. For years, she carried the weight of raising her family while grieving my abuelito and suffering from PTSD caused by the car accident.

Eventually, my mother convinced my abuelita to leave Ecuador and start over in the United States. She paid for my abuelita's one-way ticket to Miami, and we followed soon after. My mother and I came "on a vacation" when I was four years old, and 44 years later, I am still in the United States. I remember wearing an orange bikini and laying by a pool thinking I was the luckiest girl in the world. Little did I know that my mother was sitting beside me trying to figure out her next move.

We had come to the country with barely any savings, and she didn't know where we would live next. All she knew was this was her chance to begin a new life, too. She was 22 years old and a newly single mother after deciding to leave my father to come to the States.

But it was far from easy, and Miami wasn't welcoming. There were obstacles around every corner, and my mother struggled to find a job. As an undocumented immigrant, her options were limited. She tried to find childcare jobs, but every family she found wanted a live-in nanny—and didn't want that nanny to come with her own daughter in tow. Instead of sending me back to Ecuador, she decided to migrate to New York City. She made a vow to herself to never leave me behind, even though taking me would complicate her journey.

With the help of my father's sister Lillia, my abuelita, my mother, and I eventually settled in Astoria, Queens, after multiple attempts elsewhere—running from "la migra," we were displaced several times. While Tia Lillia took us under her wing, other family members had tried to sabotage our lives by reporting us to immigrations services and limiting the use of electricity in a basement apartment we rented from them in Elmhurst. Once, I had to stay perfectly silent and still in a closet while la migra searched the basement, following an anonymous tip. It was terrifying, especially because I thought I had done something wrong. That was when my mother's temperament began to change.

In the years to come, I frequently got in trouble for making noise, not cleaning, being a clumsy kid who broke things, or forgetting to do something. My mother had little patience, and her anger was frightening. When she lost her calm, she hit me so hard with a belt that she left welts on my legs. I learned the facial expressions or tone in her voice that meant she was in one of her moods, and those days, I prepared by wearing two pairs of pants. My abuelita tried to protect me from my mother's constant outbursts and would sometimes put herself in between us to keep me out of harm's way.

I've come to understand that my mother turned to physical abuse as a response to lacking control and order. Our lives were unpredictable, which was underscored by having to flee homes twice to skirt la migra (the immigration police), so my mother was obsessed with details and the things she could control. This continued for two years until my dad arrived. As much as she may have wanted to start anew, my mother's heart always brought her back to my dad. But being reunited with my father didn't erase the trauma of the last five years—the car accident that tore my family apart, migrating to a different country, displacement, fearing police officers and family separation, and my mother's abuse. No matter how much time passed, I still felt like the little girl trying to make sense of so much hurt.

Sometimes, that hurt became too heavy, and I was ready to give up. My teenage years were filled with trauma due to my dad's infidelity and my mother's anxiety. At eighteen, I was ready to leave my home. I could not take it any longer, so I applied to an out-of-state college. By then, my parents were repairing their marriage and making plans to return to Ecuador with my two younger sisters.

At nineteen, I was living alone in New York. I had just come back from West Palm Beach Atlantic College where I had failed every class and was the survivor of an unreported sexual assault. I was broke, and I had a now-useless student loan to pay back. My family had moved back to Ecuador, and I learned that one of my little sisters was also a survivor of sexual abuse. I was angry, broken, and felt like a failure. I failed school, failed to protect my sister, and blamed myself for what happened to me at college. I began to drink and cope with my anger through late nights at a bar across from my retail job.

Intoxicated one night, I took the train home alone at one in the morning. The train stopped in between stations, and I looked up to see a man with a hat sitting across from me. He walked up to me, put his hands on my head and said a prayer. I don't remember what he said, but I remember the feeling of it. I began to cry, and with every tear that fell onto my shoes, I felt lighter, hopeful, and loved. This stranger touched my soul, and as the train began to move, I looked up, and he was gone. The next morning, I asked my grandmother to describe my grandfather and what he wore the last time she saw him. She described that very same man I saw on the train. He had saved my life once again.

INSIGHT

Even though I was too proud to say anything, my parents could sense that I was struggling. They told me to come back to Ecuador, that they would take care of everything I needed. But I couldn't return to the original site of my trauma. It may have followed me to Miami and then New York, but I knew that my grandfather visiting me on the train that night was a sign that I needed to keep moving forward. I was determined to keep building my new life and break the cycle of intergenerational trauma.

I tried college again. There, I got a taste of my passion for learning about how our behaviors and triggers are due to deep-rooted, unprocessed feelings. But before I could finish my degree, I had to drop out—I couldn't even afford the train fare to get to school, much less the tuition.

So I threw myself into working in the music industry. I hadn't finished college and I had never worked in an office before, but through tireless networking, I was hired at Jive Records as a radio promotions coordinator. I moved on to WKTU as a radio promoter, and after a few years, the Motown Records' public relations department. I enjoyed my work, I was married, and it seemed like I had it all, but it was tinged with an underlying sadness.

I thought I had reached success, but I was still emotionally struggling. I was working in a charged environment that was focused on beauty, and though I was surrounded by people of color, I didn't feel like I belonged. I was in love, but something was missing. I didn't feel seen, and I didn't feel heard. I felt lost. My confidence, once a gift, was at an all-time low, and I felt deeply insecure. I couldn't have articulated it then, but I now realize that the roots of my trauma—and the burden I carried from my family's trauma—had wrapped themselves around my every bone and were getting increasingly tighter. I didn't know how, but I needed a way to set myself free.

FREEDOM

I began to open my eyes on August 27, 2000, the day my daughter was born. As tiny as she was, Isabella gave me a new perspective on life. I wanted to give her more than I ever had, so I left the music industry to spend more time with her and go back to school. I waited tables so I could finally finish my degree. Nothing was going to get in my way this time. Although my marriage fell apart, and I became a single mom when Isabella was a year old, I had more fire in me than ever before. I worked hard at being a good mother. I joined support groups for single parents in school, began my own therapy a few years later, and focused on my healing. I wanted to be kind and loving, not cause harm or trauma. I wanted to break that cycle of violence.

I remember days I would walk into the bedroom and scream into the pillows instead of losing my cool—I never hit my daughter. We grew up very close. She trusts me, and I have never let her down. She is my favorite person in the world, and I love her and respect her. I have apologized when I was wrong and was accountable to her. It was hard, and it took immense self-control to be the opposite of what I knew. I would talk about it in therapy and with other mothers, who could relate. I remember how expensive therapy was, but I was determined to heal and be better for Isabella.

By the time Isabella was ten, I graduated with my master's in social work from New York University, and by the time she was twenty-one, I owned my own business and had published my first book, Latinx In Social Work, an instant best seller. I was drawn to social work because it helped me learn about family dynamics and human behavior, including my own. Social work has given me the tools to process my trauma, beginning with healing the little one inside of me.

I confronted the inner child inundated with blame and criticism from my parents, who implied I would never be good enough. That girl grew into a social worker/entrepreneur/author/board member/general overachiever who was burning the candle at both ends and still not convinced she was good enough. So, I began to speak to my younger self with a gentleness I was unaccustomed to. I recited positive affirmations to rewire my thoughts, build secure attachments, and know that I am deserving of what I have. At first, I was afraid to talk about my childhood because I did not want to think or speak badly of my parents. But revisiting my childhood helped me see my parents as humans with their own past traumas, and forgiveness soon followed.

Forgiveness is powerful. It cleanses you and sets you free. We often move through our life burdened with baggage. We carry the weight of our ancestors' traumas and our unrepaired souls. We sabotage good relationships, live with unprocessed anger, and cause harm to ourselves and our loved ones.

I'm still unpacking my past, but I've learned countless lessons while starting to heal. Find your grit. Limit the negative self-talk. Let go of what doesn't serve you–it will only weigh you down. My success has been my healing. It has been my liberation.

FINAL THOUGHTS

We often find ourselves navigating life through a lens of obtaining wealth and power, yet when we reach it, we may still feel powerless and lost. Our journeys are filled with constant reminders of things we must work on. Some of our struggles may cause us to self-sabotage ourselves and relationships. I encourage you to ask yourself, what does success look like for me?

Is it being married and having kids? Is it a CEO title, houses, cars, and a walk-in closet? We can chase the dream and constantly catch a glimpse of hope of happiness when we obtain these landmarks, but I know too well that is not what life is all about. It's about the relationship you have with yourself. Centering in your own narrative and healing from your past traumas. It is about forgiveness of others but most importantly acceptance of your incredible magnificent power. Loving yourself is very hard and one should not be shamed for struggling to do so. Just know we are all behind you, elevating you and calling to your incredible ancestors who carried the weight of the world on their shoulders to give you a little less to carry. To be liberated.

REFLECTION QUESTIONS

1. How has the narrative of your childhood limited you in life?

2. What is your definition of success, and does it include healing?

3. How can you transform and stop the intergenerational ancestral cycle of trauma?

BIOGRAPHY

Erica Sandoval is an award-winning mental health practitioner, speaker, executive coach, entrepreneur, podcaster, philanthropist, and author of *Latinx in Social Work*, published in both English and Spanish. Most recently, she is the founder and CEO of Sandoval Psychotherapy Consulting – known as Sandoval CoLab – where she oversees a team of social workers and leads diversity, equity, and inclusion work for organizations, universities, health care facilities, medical and corporate professionals. Erica began her career in the music industry before pivoting to social work, which led her spending seven years as an advocate for children and families at the New York City Hospital for Special Surgery and working at the Make-A-Wish Foundation. During the pandemic, Erica opened her own private therapy practice.

She holds an associate's degree from the Borough of Manhattan Community College, a bachelor's degree from Baruch College, and a master's in social work from the New York University Silver School of Social Work. The recipient of many awards, Erica was recently recognized by Prospanica-NY with the 2021 Top Latinx Leaders, Social Justice award, and the Make-A-Wish Foundation gave Erica the 2018 Diversity and Inclusion Innovation award. In 2020, Erica became the first immigrant Latina president of the National Association of Social Workers' New York City chapter. Her greatest pride is being a single mother and raising her 21-year-old daughter, Isabella, whom she considers her biggest teacher. As a proud immigrant from Ecuador, her passion is fueled by supporting the community she is a part of and their children. Erica is a philanthropist and is a donor to the Latino Social Work Coalition and Scholarship Fund.

Erica Priscilla Sandoval, LCSW
www.latinxinsocialwork.com
www.sandovalcolab.com
Instagram.com/latinxinsocialwork
Instagram.com/sandovalcolab
LinkedIn: Erica Priscilla Sandoval, LCSW

Luzy D King

"You have the power to change your family's trajectory"

For nearly two decades, I was focused on climbing the corporate ladder. In 2019, I left my job after seventeen years. I am a first-gen professional and the first person in my family to hold a top executive job. I spent seventeen years working in the hospitality industry, starting as a housekeeper and then learning nearly every position throughout the company. My curiosity and ambition led me to become a general manager eventually. However, I was underpaid and overworked. Salary negotiations were not popular and whenever I prepared to "fight" for my raise, I was told the industry average was a 3% increase. All the research I've done and repeated practicing in front of a mirror to show confidence during the negotiation process disappeared in a split second. I wasn't even given the opportunity to discuss why I was worthy of earning more. My performance reviews were excellent; I was admired left and right, but my salary compensation did not reflect my corporate achievements.

After becoming a mom, I struggled to find balance. I pushed myself daily; I gave it my all to continue being the audacious leader my boss was used to. It was difficult for me, especially because I didn't have the support I needed to stay afloat. During my time as a top executive, the unemployment rate was low, and finding qualified employees was challenging. Not to mention we had a competing hotel chain coming to the area and the employees were ready for a change. I found myself working multiple positions, working longer, and when seeking help, was told to "hang in there!—We will be sending help soon." The help never arrived. My obsession with overworking and trying to prove to myself and my boss I could do it all led me to have a miscarriage. This life-changing event happened so fast, it's like a blurry memory in my mind, but still hurts. I didn't give myself the time I needed to mourn; I was too busy putting out fires at work.

A few months later, my second pregnancy was confirmed, and this time I was determined to have a sister for my oldest daughter. When sharing the news with my boss, I was confronted with an "Oh you are one of those women in the company with that problem!" I was expecting something along the lines of, "Yay, congrats!" Or the typical "When are you due?" Instead, I had become a problem because I decided to grow my family. I knew it was time for me to leave, especially when this unwelcomed comment was made in front of the VP of Human Resources, and the only reaction was, "He's just kidding."

I left an industry that was all I knew at the time. I had to discover my own path. It was one of the scariest things I've done: I was leaving my dream career and a position I worked hard to obtain.

REINVENTION BEGINS

I put myself back in school to earn my MBA while transitioning as a stay-at-home mom. While pursuing my MBA, I learned more about the stock market and investing through one of my finance classes. As I started learning more about investing, I began to question why the fundamentals of money management weren't ever taught to me. The topics of how I could build wealth as a first-gen were never taught to me at home or in school. I didn't even have a clear understanding of how my previous employer's retirement plan worked. My bank account and finances did not reflect my hard work of seventeen years. I was working hard for my money and not letting my money work for me, all due to my lack of financial literacy.

I felt shame and blamed myself for not knowing how to manage my money and pay myself first. But how could I? Money was such a big taboo topic in my household growing up and still is in our community. So, I started to seek answers and dive deep into learning everything I could about investing, money management, the psychology of money, the systems wealthy people use to create wealth.

I made it my mission to become the first investor in my family, break generational chains of poverty, and unlearn my money story: the story of overworking until we no longer can, the narrative that if you don't work hard, you are lazy! After researching the gender gap and the wealth gap I decided to focus on teaching Latinas and WOC everything I was doing to create systems for their money.

WHEN YOU DON'T HAVE ENOUGH

In 2020 while watching the news on TV, I witnessed how many women, mainly Latina women, were losing their jobs because of COVID. It shocked me to learn that most of those women didn't have an emergency fund to provide the financial stability they needed after losing their jobs. A lack of financial literacy was affecting the entire nation.

A few months before the pandemic hit, I was denied financial advice because I didn't have $100K to start investing and was even told most financial planners don't seek women of color as clients. If you are a first-gen professional or immigrant, there is a high probability you don't have that kind of money lying around the house or under the mattress. Let that sink in for a moment! Most Financial Planners won't take clients unless they have $100K to start investing. Does this sound right to you? A few months later, I learned you can start investing with as little as $5.00.

When interviewing a second financial planning firm, I was legitimately curious to know how many clients they were serving who were Latino or people of color. I was told they have zero. Being the inquisitive person I am, I asked, "why?" The answer I got: "we just don't seek those demographics." I was told their firm doesn't have anybody who speaks Spanish. They also mentioned being too busy with their non-Hispanic clients.

I took the risk to launch an online financial literacy agency and coaching business to bridge the Latinx wealth gap and the Latina Wage Gap.

Coming from a corporate background and having studied business, I was constantly encouraged to have a business plan, a sales plan, a marketing plan, but I didn't have all of those plans fully developed yet. However, I did have a passion and commitment to teaching others how financial literacy and investing are the key to financial stability. So, I took the risk to share my story online, even though I was raised to be a private person and never talk about money matters in public.

FINDING MY PURPOSE

This risk let me find my purpose. I run my dream business from home, and I have the time to prioritize my health and be a great mom. I wake up thinking, "who am I going to serve today?" rather than, "what kind of problem am I going to face today?"

I am no longer putting out "fires" or feeling stressed about asking for a 3% raise. Instead, I am showing up authentically, serving Latinas, and creating my income. Sometimes, it feels unreal that I am having money conversations with other Latinas and WOC when I was constantly told, "calladita te ves más bonita," "shut up and look prettier." Together, we are embracing our money story, creating the money systems that will allow us to create a life beyond our ancestors' wildest dreams.

I have time to think about the long-term impact of embracing my new purpose. I think about my clients and all the people they are impacting by sharing their money conversations. I think about our community and the importance of representation in an industry that wasn't made for us. I think about the children in our community, including my daughters, and the abundance-mentality they are being raised in.

Success is not linear, and I encourage you, Mujer, to take a risk. Follow your passion and stay committed, you have what it takes to create the life your ancestors couldn't dream of because they were too busy trying to survive. Start before you are ready. Start now.

REFLECTION QUESTIONS

1. When was the last time you took a risk?

2. Who is holding you back from taking a risk?

3. What steps do you need to take to create your dream life?

BIOGRAPHY

Luzy D King is a Latina Financial and Business coach, speaker and host of say Hola Wealth podcast. She has reinvented her career and found her true purpose after a career breakup. She is an advocate for closing the Latinx Wealth Gap and helping bridge the Latina Wage Gap.

In 2021, Creative Human Official recognized her as a "Power of Women Honoree" for her resilience and dedication to improving her career by opening my business in spite of a global pandemic. Luzy takes pride in her community by volunteering at a local club whose mission is to empower women and girls with access to the education and training needed to achieve economic empowerment.

Luzy is an outdoor enthusiast and enjoys cycling, running and hiking. During the winter season, Luzy enjoys skiing and sledding with her two young girls and husband. Luzy is not a fan of cooking but she is determined to learn and create new recipes for her family. Luzy is married to an amazing man who supports her wildest dreams.

Luzy is looking forward to completing her CPF certification. Luzy does not want to manage your money, she wants to teach you how to manage your money. Luzy's dream is to continue to grow the online community of ambitious, healthy and wealthy Latinas.

Luzy D King
IG: @vivalabudgetandfinance
Hello@vivalabudgetandfinance.com

Ana Larrea-Albert

"The purpose of life is a life of purpose." Robert Byrne

What is my purpose? This question has captured many of my waking hours and forces me to pause and gift myself the time for self-reflection. Not long ago, I came across the idea of *ikigai*. *Ikigai* is an ancient Japanese concept that one could interpret as "reason for being." A famous Venn diagram depicts ikigai as various dimensions of meaning overlapping to reach the sweet spot of one's ikigai, one's purpose. I find it impactful because it incorporates multiple dimensions for exploration, from the personal aspects of what one loves and is good at to the larger scope of what the world needs and finds valuable. The union of my mission, passion, vocation, and profession has become a powerful guide to reach my current purpose: to empower myself and others to live to the highest potential and make a difference in the world.

When I introduce myself, I say that I like to think of myself as multi-passionate, which means that I enjoy doing various things. I consult with organizations to help create positive change. I coach high-potential leaders to ignite their transformation and growth. I mentor students and professionals to maximize their success. I speak to and lead workshops with audiences large and intimate to catalyze "aha" moments. I also write bilingual children's books to encourage our youngest leaders to dream big and act. They may vary, but they are all driven by my purpose.

This purpose was the catalyst for me to quit my executive-level role of Vice President of Marketing and Customer Experience after almost a decade at a European multinational to return to school. I wanted to equip myself even further in the discipline of leadership, so I pursued a Master's in Public Administration at Harvard, from where I graduated in May 2021. As a result, I am now immensely fortunate to fully dedicate my time to creating an impact through my work.

This discovery of my *ikigai* is a very recent development, however. For a long time, I felt uncertain about my future and wondered whether what I was doing was helping me on my path.

I like to talk about my career as the times B.C. and A.C.: Before Coaching and After Coaching. I do this because of the powerful transformation I underwent when I received executive coaching about ten years ago. That exercise put me on the path towards true servant leadership.

TEARS ON THE ELEVATOR

Before coaching, I took the jobs I could get. I based my decisions on need. As a recent marketing graduate from Florida Atlantic University (FAU) who was on a student visa after immigrating to Florida from Quito, Ecuador, a couple of years earlier, I needed a company willing to sponsor me to continue working in the country. We left Ecuador under difficult political circumstances. Our lives were turned upside down, and the dust was starting to settle.

In my search for a work "home," I interned at an investment firm and then worked at a national bank as a teller, but neither of those institutions could sponsor me. Finally, with a looming deadline for the visa, my first and most crucial supporter arrived at my teller station in the form of a customer making that week's cash deposit. Her name was Maria, and since we were both from Ecuador, we found something in common and became friends. Our friendship grew as we continued to see each other every Friday, and when I shared my struggle to find a workplace willing to help me with a work visa, she jumped at the opportunity to make it happen. In a matter of weeks, I resigned from the bank and started working as the credit manager's assistant at the company where she worked, and thanks to their willingness to give me a chance, I was able to apply and be granted a work visa. I worked there for a few years, during which time I met my future husband and gave birth to my beautiful boy, Louie.

I continued looking and finding jobs by need, location, or schedule from that point forward. I worked as a financial coordinator, operations coordinator, marketing specialist, online marketing assistant, account manager, account executive, marketing and sales representative, and maybe another role I might have forgotten. I worked in bridal, import-export, trade shows, construction, retail, advertising, digital marketing, medical devices, and others. However, when I worked at the digital marketing agency, I felt the enormous emotional impact bad leadership could have for the first time.

Every day, on the elevator going up to the top floor, I felt fear, confusion, frustration, guilt, helplessness. But one day, I couldn't hold back my tears. I had many years of work experience already, so I wasn't new to the ups and downs of work life. Some days are good, some not so good. It happens, and you deal with it. However, the animosity I felt towards me from my supervisor overwhelmed me daily. Her demeaning comments, the incompetence of the company's top management, and the fear of being stuck without a future in that place got the best of me that day. I lost confidence in my decisions, abilities, and courage to speak up. Looking back, I know it had nothing to do with me and everything to do with my supervisor. I will never know what triggered her to treat me like that, but at that moment, I realized that a positive and empowering leader would never act in that way. Despite the emotional pain and the consequent long healing process, that moment was when my quest for understanding authentic leadership began.

THE IMMENSE VALUE OF SELF-DISCOVERY AND SELF-AWARENESS

After I decided that I had given the job a fair chance and being in that toxic environment was damaging my mental health, I quit. I felt lost. My bright, upbeat, curious self was nowhere to be found. I had made the very wrong decision to join that company, so I was having trouble trusting my instincts and put a pause on looking for another corporate job. I freelanced for friendly clients on my terms but wasn't sure where to go next.

The one thing I knew for sure was that I was good at school. I also knew that if I wanted to advance in my career towards my colossal ambition of becoming a Latina CEO of a Fortune 500 company, a Master's in Business Administration would help. I was shooting for the stars but was happy if I could land on a treetop. I know there are multiple paths to grow in one's career that don't necessarily include higher education. Still, I realized that the jobs I was getting reflected both what I believed my capabilities were and what the market found valuable in my skills. Going back to school felt like a safe anchor in that moment of disorientation.

I went back to FAU as it is close to where we lived. Despite thoroughly enjoying the classes and taking advantage of all the fantastic resources in the program, my most fortunate decision was to have selected an elective course on leadership that included executive coaching. Through the assessments and development work I did with the guidance of my coach, I was able to discover a vast world of meaning beyond my ambitious search for the next big title, which led me further down my path towards servant leadership.

My curiosity, openness, and willingness to learn came back in droves and allowed me to discover my traits, behaviors, strengths, areas of development, values, and much more. It was the first time I was genuinely looking inwards for growth. I was excited to push my capacity for development. Since that class, I have updated my personal development plan every year and given myself the chance to dream big and act towards those dreams.

WHY NOT ME?

That was my B.C., Before Coaching, experience. My After Coaching phase looked and felt completely different. And it was all thanks to one result in one assessment: my helper trait was mature, but I hadn't activated it yet. This interpretation meant that I had a strong, innate desire to help others, but I hadn't tapped into it yet.

Many journal entries and discussions with my coach later, things started to make sense, and it all came together with one change of perspective, the dismantling of a paradigm. For many years, I kept hearing about how having a mentor who cared was a key to a successful career. I had looked for that magical fairy godparent that would put me under their wing and groom me to be the next Fortune 500 CEO. It never happened. I had approached a couple of people and tried to develop a mentoring relationship with them, but they were either unavailable to be efficient or not the type who should be a mentor at all. So, I kept thinking, why can't I find someone willing to help me? Was I not good enough? Why not me?

It is easy for me to see now that I had unknowingly adopted the victim mentality. The blinders were on, and I could not see past these self-limiting beliefs. However, I committed to activating my helper trait, and I found myself making a 180-degree change. I went from demanding a mentor, a sponsor, a more prominent title—always focusing on me and what I wanted—to realizing that I could be that mentor for someone else.

Feeling delighted with this insight and unsure of what to

do about it, I decided to start by creating a platform to shine the spotlight on exceptional Latina professionals. I wanted to show the world how talented, capable, competent, educated, and ready the Latina professional community in the U.S. is to step into leadership roles. I wanted to lift my community's stories and profiles, raise awareness of the lack of Latina representation at the highest levels of corporate America, and do something to move the needle. I wanted to contribute towards positive change and make a difference in the world. I also went back to my alma mater, FAU, and offered my time to build a mentoring program for Latina students. And so, my journey in servant leadership began to take shape. During my time interviewing these amazing Latinas for the Latina Leadership Collective and working with inspiring students in the Future Latina Leaders program, I was able to articulate the first iteration of my purpose: to empower myself by empowering others. This statement assured me that only by helping others succeed I could achieve my own success. It became about others and how they could achieve their goals.

Through these experiences, I gained a standard, a filter through which I see the world that allowed me to feel more in control and at peace with future career decisions. I found my *ikigai*.

LIVING MY IKIGAI

I encourage everyone to read Simon Sinek's book "Start with Why." He states that once you've done the hard work of discovering and clearly articulating your why, your purpose, your *ikigai*, "you need to have the courage and discipline to use it."

Once I realized my purpose, every initiative I have started, every decision I have made has gone through this filter. Knowing that this filter is true to me makes me confident that my choices will be authentic and valuable. It has also become easier to say "no" without feeling guilty about it.

Once I started applying my filter and living my purpose, I realized I no longer wanted to become the CEO of a Fortune 500 company. It was a worthy goal for B.C. Ana, but all of a sudden, it became less urgent. I no longer felt that my value as a professional was tied to a big title. I was starting to make meaning in a different way. I began to change the narrative in my head, and I wanted to make a dent in the world. I remember hearing this definition of a billionaire: a billionaire is not someone with a billion dollars in their bank account but someone who has positively impacted a billion people. That definition is a much worthier goal.

Finally, and just as importantly, it's OK if you don't know what your purpose is yet. We all have our *ikigai*, that powerful intersection of passion, talent, and value to others. However, it is only through time, introspection, self-discovery, and the discomfort of growth that we can reach it. The key is to get to a point when all the dots start to connect. Steve Jobs said, "You can't connect the dots looking forward; you can only connect them looking backward. So, you have to trust that the dots will somehow connect in your future."

If you find yourself a bit adrift, not knowing your purpose yet, trust that all the experiences you are going through are building a repository of references and learnings that will come together in a powerful way. Trust that the dots will connect. It is also OK if your purpose changes in time. The more insight you gain about yourself through deep self-reflection and the more skills and capabilities you develop, along with changes in our environment, the more refined your purpose will become. So, have patience and compassion for yourself, knowing that the dots will eventually connect and that everything you are doing now is helping you weave the beautiful tapestry of your life. Your *ikigai* will patiently wait for you to discover it.

REFLECTION QUESTIONS

1. How often do you give yourself the gift of deep self-reflection?
2. How can you bring your mission, passion, vocation, and profession together to discover your purpose?
3. How have you used your experiences and lessons in your life to enrich and guide others?

BIOGRAPHY

Ana is a woman full of energy and joy who uses every opportunity to grow. She is an author, speaker, leadership expert, executive coach, mentor, and award winner. A visionary leader who has great inner strength and determination, Ana is passionate about helping others transform their lives.

After a twenty-plus year career in business, she left her executive-level role of VP, Marketing and Customer Experience to better equip herself in leadership and management sciences, graduating in 2021 from Harvard University with an MPA. Ana also has an MBA in International Business and a BS in Marketing from Florida Atlantic University (FAU), and is a certified Organization Development Professional.

She is the creator of several mentoring and coaching programs, is well known as the founder of the Latina Leadership Collective, and she authored the bilingual children's book series "ZeeZee Can" that encourages children to dream big.

Her work with the Hispanic community was recognized with the Latina of Influence distinction and the Everyday Hero Award nomination. She has presented on leadership and Latinx empowerment in the US and abroad.

Ana was born in Quito, Ecuador, and lives in Florida, with her husband, son, and puppy, ZeeZee, the inspiration for her book series.

Ana Larrea-Albert
ana@analarreaalbert.com
LinkedIn: /anaalbert
Instagram: @analarreaalbert
@latinaleadershipcollective

Rocio Alejandra Carroll

"Once you achieve your dreams, do not forget to pay it forward, add value to others, develop leaders around you, and lead the way."

My journey in search of my purpose and the fulfillment of my biggest dream began in August of 1993. I was still living in my beautiful city of Morelia, Michoacan, México where I was born on a cold Christmas day. I was studying Architecture at the University of San Nicolas de Hidalgo, had only one more semester, and my thesis left to graduate and be certified as an Architect. I am the oldest of four sisters and the one my mother relied on after becoming a single mom of three teenagers and a newborn. My parents separated only a few months after my fifteenth birthday celebration and resulted in a family crisis that started years earlier. In our home, my sisters and I were kept in the dark about the problems between my parents. We had limited information about the political and the economic challenges my parents were facing after the depression in Mexico during the '80s. It all came to us at once, when the problems could no longer be hidden. My parents announced the possible cancellation of my birthday celebration, only a couple of weeks ahead of Christmas; a party they had planned and prepared for about three years. All of the invitations were sent two months in advance and our family from the U.S. had made their travel plans. Most of the invitations were for politicians, bureaucratics in educational institutions, and government officials; my father's circle of influence. As the firstborn, this type of celebration was expected as an introduction to society. Turning fifteen signified a transition from a teenager into adulthood and the party intended to establish a network that would help shape my future. They asked what I intended to study, some seemed disappointed when I said I wanted to study fashion or graphic design. The majority of people within their circle of influence were accountants, engineers, architects, college and university professors, and a few doctors. To my parents and their acquaintances, graphic design was a form of art, and I would not be able to make a living out of that career, so they encouraged me to pursue architecture instead. Since my parents would not allow me to study outside my city I had only two choices, study architecture at a private school or a public university. The difference between the two, other than the tuition, was that the degree from the private university was not recognized outside of my state. So I elected to go to the Universidad Michoacana De San Nicolás De Hidalgo because I did not want to be limited to work in my city. I wanted to spread my wings to fly as high as I could.

In August of 1993, I made the first decision of my own without letting anyone know about my plans. I came to California with my grandmother to "visit for a month" before going back to school; however, my plan, my desire, my biggest dream was to attend a university in the U.S. where I will be able to have more career options. I thought it was going to be easy with no idea of the journey ahead. I only knew I was going to accomplish my dream at all costs. For the longest time I wanted to make my own decisions without the help or influence of my parents. I was given too much responsibility as a teenager and felt I had no rights. My voice was often ignored and I had no choice but to accept their decisions.

LANGUAGE, EVERY IMMIGRANT'S STUMBLING BLOCK

As it is the case for most immigrants from Latin America, one of my first challenges was the language barrier. Although I had a university-level education and a solid cultural foundation, I was not able to communicate which was very frustrating. I had trouble ordering food at a restaurant, and asking for directions was incomprehensible as not everyone spoke Spanish. How was I able to accomplish my goal if I could not communicate nor comprehend the language? I studied English not only at school as part of the curriculum, but I attended an institute just to learn the language. I scheduled an appointment with the school counselor where I enrolled in English level 1 a couple of months after my arrival. His advice was to stop watching TV in Spanish and instead watch cartoons and try to understand the language based on the characters' body language. I used graphics as a communication tool to make up for the words I did not know how to translate to English. I became a professional at pictograms, like from the caveman era. I always wondered why there were a lot of Latinos who had lived in the US for a long time but could not speak the language. I noticed that on multiple occasions it was fear, shame, lack of confidence that paralyzed and prevented people from learning or continuing to learn the language. I was determined to improve so I would not find myself in the same situation years later. I had to overcome my fear, my insecurities and needed to remind myself that I had an education as a backup. I was so close to becoming an architect in Mexico, not knowing the language was not going to stop me from achieving my dream. I had to work harder, study longer hours, and stay focused on my goal, not on my limitations. I asked my parents to send me the best Spanish-English dictionary from Mexico. A Larousse dictionary, a set of blank cards, my college books, and hyphenated class notes became the most important tools at the beginning of my college education journey. I enrolled at Los Angeles Valley College during the Spring semester of 1998. As I was waiting to enter the classroom, I was frightened by all the student conversations. I waited in fear, doubting if I was going to be able to understand the teacher and doubting I was going to be able to pass the class. I took notes as I was able to comprehend the sounds and words; most of my notes were illegible. At the end of the class, I spoke with the professor to let her know I was dropping her course. When she asked me why, I showed her my notes. How was I going to be able to pass when 50% of the grade consisted of three essay questions? She took my notebook, read it, asked a couple of questions, and said to me, "I can understand what you wrote, so why don't you wait until after the first quiz and decide then what to do?" Her answer gave me some reassurance. I figured there was nothing for me to lose and this could be an opportunity to test my skills. I went home that day and translated my notes into blank cards with the use of my dictionary, my book, and I asked my husband to help me make sense of some of the words I wrote based on the sounds. I repeated this process every day after class and to my relief, I passed the first quiz with a B. I met with the professor again and asked her for feedback. She encouraged me to continue. If I could do the same thing at every quiz and test I would have no problem passing her class. In the end, I obtained an A in her class. This boosted my confidence to another level and I continued to apply the same process in subsequent classes. In my second semester, I took my first English class. I was placed into the ESL (English as a Second Language) curriculum. It was not until the 2000 Spring Semester when I was able to enroll in English 101 Honors where the average High School Freshman–Sophomore typically starts at college. By then I made the Dean's List both as a part-time and full-time student as well as the President Honors List. In May of 2000, I was recognized by Phi Theta Kappa, the International Scholastic Order of the Two Year College, and my name was published in a nationwide book. My dream was taking shape, it was becoming a reality.

WHEN YOU DREAM BIG TRUST GOD FOR A MIRACLE AND DO NOT GIVE UP

Not everyone supported me. Many discouraged me along the way, especially because at the same time that I was going to school I was raising a family. My first son was born in 1995 just three years before I started college, followed by the birth of my daughter in 1996. Having a childcare facility within the campus was a blessing. As soon as my children turned four years old and were potty trained I was able to take them to the school daycare while I was in class. There were a few occasions when I had to pick them up and had no other choice but to take them with me to class. I did not want to miss class and as long as they were behaving the professors had no problem with my children. That flexibility and support are what parents need, not only in a school setting but in the workplace whenever possible. Being a parent or a single parent should not be considered a handicap.

In 2001, I was admitted to the University of Southern California as well as to Cal Poly Pomona, UCLA, and UC Santa Cruz. Out of all, USC was the only one that had a bachelor's in Architecture. I was one of fifteen transferred students accepted into the School of Architecture. I was beyond happy and grateful to God for His favor and blessing. I had not only received several scholarships upon graduation from Los Angeles Valley College but financial aid covered all of my tuition. With all of the scholarship checks I received, I was able to cover immediate expenses, including rent. God was showing me He was my provider as most of those scholarships were unexpected and the financial aid package was going to help subsidize some of our housing expenses. I could not give up, not then, not now, not ever.

I attended USC for five years, along the way God gave me favor with my peers and my professors; He kept me afloat financially, spiritually, and gave me the capacity to continue learning while raising four small children. God provided opportunities for employment after my graduation in 2006 without having to knock on too many doors. I started working as an intern project engineer in 2003 for a General Contractor in downtown LA, where I worked on a diverse range of commercial projects and by 2006 I had a job offer. Always seeking options, I chose to stay in construction as I enjoyed my internship and wanted to learn how to build. The diversity of projects I have been part of has allowed me to continue learning not only about architecture and construction, but about people, leadership, processes, organizations, teams, and the culture within an organization. In 2011, I became a founding partner of the John Maxwell Team and in 2013, a certified leadership coach. Since then I have been studying everything about leadership and its importance in every aspect of our lives. As John Maxwell says "Everything rises and falls on leadership". It is essential for you and me to lead our lives, to continue to grow, to expand our capacity, and to not settle with the limitations that others place in our lives just because of our national origin, skin color, gender, sexual orientation, age, marital status, parenthood, accent, upbringings, or our socio-economic status, etc. Through my journey in life, I have learned to count my blessings, to get up every time I fell, to learn from my failures and shortcomings, to not give in, and not give up. I encourage you to stay focused on your goal and do not let the current circumstances distract you to the point that you lose sight of your dream. As Dr. Martin Luther King said in his speech, 'I Have a Dream' under the freedom symbolized by the flag of this nation and under those precepts of equality all men are created equal. I encourage you to do your best to break every stereotype and adjective that states that we, the minorities in this country, are not capable of accomplishing our dreams. Dream big, do not let anyone discourage you or tell you what you can or cannot do. Look up, focus on your goals, take action, acknowledge your successes, learn from your mistakes, if you fall, if you fail, get up and do it again, and again, and again. As a person of faith, I believe prayer is the key that changes everything for the good, consistency, determination, courage, passion also known as purpose gives us strength to push against the current until we get a breakthrough; the sacrifice will be worth it in the end. Once you achieve your dreams, do not forget to pay it forward, add value to others, develop leaders around you, and lead the way.

REFLECTION QUESTIONS

1. What have I learned so far?

2. What will be the heritage I leave behind?

3. How can I be a voice and leader for those who feel invisible?

BIOGRAPHY

Rocio Carroll was born in Morelia, Michoacán, Mexico, where she studied architecture before immigrating to the United States in August of 1993. Her biggest dream was to pursue a career at a prestigious American university, but she knew it wasn't going to be easy as she didn't know what or how long it would take her. She pushed herself hard and had to learn a new language, adjust to a new culture, and maintain a positive attitude regardless of the circumstances she encountered. She learned English and her journey led her to the University of Southern California where she studied architecture from 2001-2006.

In 2003, Rocio started her internship in construction where she had the opportunity to utilize her architectural skills combined with technology and it became the perfect niche and the specialization of her career of over 20 years. The combination of design, construction, and technology is what most people within the Architecture, Engineering, and Construction (AEC Industry), know as Building Information Modeling (BIM) or Virtual Design and Construction. Rocio took every opportunity available to expand her knowledge and learned from every project she worked on to develop a deeper understanding of construction. Her expertise and skills added value to the teams and diverse stakeholders within her projects through collaboration, visual communication, constructability analysis, integration of public safety, operations, construction, and project logistics for internal planning.

While studying architecture in Mexico, Rocio learned that as an architect she is responsible for the safety and wellbeing of all those clients who will benefit from her projects. She is keen on attention to detail and believes precision is a key element to a safe and successful project. As John Maxwell says, "Everything rises and falls on leadership." As a leader in her field, Rocio is proud to ensure the safety of current and future occupants of the buildings and public safety during and after construction.

Rocio Alejandra Carroll
JRCGlobalEnterprisesLLC@gmail.com
Instagram: @MexiCanDream91
LinkedIn: Rocio Carroll (Rocio Alejandra García)

Sandra Keys

"Self-discovery often happens when we move out of our comfort zone and change the norm" – Fola O'Martins

WHY ME?

It's the Monday after Christmas, the holiday rush has dissipated, and everyone is anticipating the arrival of a new year. "New Year, new me" mentality is already at the top of everyone's social media campaigns. Not mine. I was embarking on a whole new journey that had me asking myself, "Why me?" I couldn't wrap my thoughts around the fact that I was about to spend New Year's Eve, in Puerto Vallarta, sad and alone. It was never in my plans. My New Years was meant to be spent in Colombia, nestled up in the mountains of Medellin, in the arms of my significant other. In my eyes, everything was perfect—but the sad reality was I was living a fantasy all on my own. We were together for four years; it was a long-distance relationship that required us to split our time amongst Chicago and Colombia. The beginning years were great, I truly enjoyed Colombia and envisioned myself even living there during the winter months. It wasn't until I was on my way back to Colombia in early December that something felt off when I arrived. The vibe wasn't right, and I could sense the tension in the room. After a few days, I decided it was best for me to walk away. I grabbed my bags, booked my flight back home and did not look back. My heart was in pieces and my mind was in a fog. I didn't know what to feel, nor what to think. I kept second guessing my decision, "Did I overreact by leaving? Should I have stayed?" It was during this mental battlefield that I decided I needed to get away, even if that meant going alone. I never imagined traveling by myself; it felt strange. That sense of knowing that at the other side, there would be no one waiting for me felt like an empty pit in my stomach.

THE FLIGHT

I kept swallowing my tears, forcing a smiling façade, and coaching myself mentally through the whole process. I am at the airport, watching families and couples rush to their gates, businesspeople probably trying to catch the next flight home to be reunited with their families–it was a lot to take in and brought me sadness. I decided before boarding that plane that I would utilize this time alone to reflect and silence the outside noise. Rather than focus on solidarity, I would shift my mindset and embrace the season. With that mindset—I boarded my flight and my journey began. My four-hour plane ride would prepare me to recover the pieces of myself that I didn't even know I had lost. It was all found within the pages of a book that my daughter gave me prior to my trip titled, *Uninvited* by Lysa TerKeurst. This book was a key element in my healing process. It taught me how to receive love. My entire life, I have always been the giver. For me, giving to others filled me with such joy. But when it came for me to sit back and allow others to give to me, I rejected it. I learned that by doing so, I was only robbing others from that same joy that I felt. This book taught me that it's okay to allow others in and to break down that barrier that I created years ago, out of fear of rejection. After finishing the book on the plane, I realized that this trip symbolized the beginning of allowing myself to receive what came my way. In doing so, when I walked off that plane, I released full control and said, "Enjoy the journey and be willing to receive whatever God has in store for your life". On the trolley ride to the resort, I met two amazing women who saw the sadness behind my eyes. The outpouring of love they bestowed on me marked me for the days to come. This was my first test, and because I was open to being vulnerable, I allowed them to embrace me with an open heart. I saw the genuine joy it gave them to treat me to dinner and it felt good to be on the other side receiving that joy.

A LITTLE BIT OF SUNSHINE

The next morning, the sun was shining, and the ocean breeze brought a smile to my face. How amazing to be able to wake up to such beauty, it was breathtaking. In those moments of solidarity, I truly learned to admire every detail around me: the sound of the waves as they rippled the sand, the birds chirping in the distance, the iguanas that would roam around the tree branches, and the stillness in the silence. Often, we allow the distractions around us to rob us of the experience because we are more in tune with the outside noise. So, I decided that this trip I would focus solely on the experience. I began journaling daily and filling my mind with positivity. I listened to motivational podcasts and started reflecting each morning on the things I was grateful for. I blocked out all news outlets and concentrated on my introspection. I wanted to be intentional and remove any negative energy from entering my mind. I needed to cleanse my mind and spirit.

So, my five-day getaway turned into a one-month sabbatical of finding myself again. I had to first let go and let God. Once I did that, He began ordering my steps. Every person that crossed my path during this journey was placed there for a purpose. I met some amazing people with powerful stories. Amongst the friendships made, there were two women that took me under their wings and made me feel safe enough to be raw. I was like an onion, never allowing anyone to get close enough to begin peeling away the layers of emotion, simply out of fear. I feared allowing anyone to see me down. My personality has always been to be the "strong" woman no matter the circumstance, which is why this task was so difficult for me. I have always been one to freeze my emotions. I have even been called "ice queen" in the past. But this trip taught me that it is okay to be vulnerable because to be vulnerable allows room to grow and heal. This season I was forced to allow those layers to be peeled away with love, which is what these women showed me. They were filled with such inspiration that it was contagious. They taught me that we have a daily choice to be happy. We are in control of that emotion, and we cannot allow our circumstances to determine our happiness. Life is messy but we have the choice to get up and try again. We are our biggest critic; We must get out of our own head and walk with confidence, daily. These women empowered me to think differently.

THOUGHT LIFE

My thoughts have always been difficult to navigate. It is almost as if my mind had a mind of its own. It would never stop. During my stay, I decided to go outside of my comfort zone and host a meditation seminar for three days with six strangers. It was a powerful experience that I highly recommend. I had to put into practice being vulnerable and sharing my heart. Being vulnerable meant sharing my heartbreak with them. It meant allowing them to know details that felt embarrassing. For any woman sharing about a breakup can feel debilitating. We can feel worthless and not worthy to be loved. It can make us question so many different aspects about ourselves. The best part about the healing process was accepting myself for who I am designed to be while giving myself the grace to grow. Our greatness and ability to be loved should not be measured by any other being but ourselves. This part of my journey brought great healing to my inner thoughts. I began truly putting into practice self-love and the importance of being true to who I am as a woman. I began meditating on my own and found so much comfort in the silence.

GROWTH

Each day was a new adventure, all because these strangers opened themselves up to me and graced me with love. They allowed me the space to open my heart and share my story. They loved me at my worst without even knowing me, and they showed me how to be at my best. I was in a season of deep sadness. I walked around feeling unworthy, not enough and defeated at love. If it weren't for their friendship and support, I wouldn't have had the strength to lift myself out of that hole all on my own. They were that helping hand that pushed me through and helped me shift my mindset and begin my healing process. I believe that everything that transpired happened just the way it was supposed to happen and although it was painful, I believe I came out stronger. I would have never had this outcome, had I not read Lysa TerKeurst's book which allowed me to be open to receiving all this love; it prepared my heart to receive. We don't realize that the simplest thing like a book can have so much power. We must seek those self-help resources that are available to us in order to and flourish as women.

Now, I go back to that question that I asked myself at the beginning of my journey, "Why me?", and I find that I was asking the wrong question. Instead, the question was, "What are you teaching me?" You see, God knew exactly what I needed, and through my sadness, I gained so much. I learned to be secure enough to eat alone, with no distractions, simply observing everything around me. I learned to silence my mind and meditate. I learned that I was worthy to be loved and to receive from others. Best of all, I learned that underneath it all, was a woman who needed to lose control of her emotions to gain control of herself again. I arrived empty and left full and ready to receive whatever comes next.

REFLECTION QUESTIONS

1. Where in your life do you need clarity?

2. Do you find yourself struggling with fear or opening yourself up to being vulnerable with others?

3. How can you create daily space to be intentional about working on self-love?

BIOGRAPHY

Sandra Keys is a Latina of Colombian descent who spends her time helping people obtain the dream of homeownership. Sandra has been a Loan Officer for 30 years now and enjoys every moment of what she does. Her powerhouse team is made up of 4 amazing Latina women who are passionate, driven and go getters. The assembly of this team has taken years to find, and she is extremely grateful to finally have all the elements needed to serve people. When Sandra is not working, she enjoys seeking adventure, traveling, embracing the outdoors, and cooking. She has two wonderful children, a son and a daughter. She is honored to say that her daughter is the right hand of her business. It truly has been a joy for Sandra working side by side with her and sharing this legacy with her. Together they have managed to grow and continue growing and learning daily.

She is honored to share her story with others, especially in this book, and she hopes that in reading it, it can help at least one woman in whatever season they may be in.

Sandra Keys
630-854-9760
skeys@loandepot.com
Instagram: @sk_thekeysteam

Isabel Ramirez

"Some people come into our lives as blessings.
Some come in your life as lessons."
–Mother Teresa

Did you grow up knowing what you wanted to do with your life, or who you were going to be? Was it easy to decide on a career path? In third grade, I knew I wanted to be an attorney. I wanted to wear suits and high heels. My favorite shows were about attorneys and court cases. I dreamt of being in a courtroom! In high school, I would wear suits to school because I was dressing like the lawyer I wanted to be. I was so sure of what I was going to do. I had my whole life planned out...until I didn't.

THE DREAM BEGINS

I was born in Mexico and came to the United States when I was six years old. My parents were not formally educated, so their dream was for us to be first-generation college graduates. My family could not afford to pay for college, so I took advantage of two years of free college education on a Merit scholarship from Moraine Valley Community College. Paying for two more years of college and law school on my own was going to be hard. Back then, I didn't have anyone to guide me. Were my dreams of becoming a lawyer slipping away? I was not giving up! Keep going, I would tell myself every morning. You can do this! Finish these two years, and you'll find a way to pay for your education—there are always loans.

I completed two years at the junior college and transferred to St. Xavier University. I chose this University based on geography, it was close to my job, and I was determined to graduate! I enjoyed my time there and made a lot of friends. As young adults often do, we would talk about our dreams and career goals. The business and education majors were always deliberating as to why their field was a better option. We went back and forth as if we were going to convince the other person to change their major—especially the ones that wanted to be teachers. I know, it was a hefty goal. I remember the conversations as if they were yesterday. We, the international business majors, said we were going to travel around the world and work for an international company. The future teachers would have nothing of it. They were convinced they would make a difference in children's lives and touch the future, " Teachers make every career possible, they are instrumental in all of our lives". Blah, Blah, Blah was all we heard! The business students all agreed that the classroom was not a place for us. We could not see ourselves taking care of children! A similar conversation would take place several times before we all graduated. It was amusing for all of us! We were so sure of where our paths were headed, and it was certainly not working as a teacher!

THE CHALLENGE BEGINS

I planned to graduate with a major in International Business, a minor in Spanish, and then go on to law school. But the universe would have a different plan for my future.

As the end of my senior year approached I had to find another job, and buy a car. I was so proud of myself to find the perfect job for this situation as a car salesperson.

I was so close to graduating! As luck would have it, the two courses I needed to graduate were not offered until the following school year. So what was I going to do now? I was going backward and farther away from my dreams. My friend Teresa, who had graduated that May, recommended me for the position she didn't take. A full-time job was exactly what I needed! I got the job, and now I was eager to finish my degree as soon as the courses I needed were offered. What seemed like an easy task took two more years to finish.

I started working as a receptionist for a foreign governmental agency. My job was to assist the directors of the sports, community relations, and education departments. Our education department assisted individuals with obtaining their credentials to help them apply for their teaching certificates in the United States. I even had the opportunity to translate their transcripts. At that time, due to a teacher shortage, the State of Illinois had a temporary certificate for people with a bachelor's degree. Miguel Sanchez was our contact person and he was instrumental in helping the teachers register for the required proficiency language tests. Miguel would often encourage me to take the proficiency test and become a teacher. A teacher, me? Never! Not in a million years! I declined his offer every time. After all, I still held on to my dream of going to law school. Why would I give that up?

Miguel kept insisting, until I caved in and said, "Yes—I will take the exam". I figured this was the only way he would stop asking me. He set up the test rather quickly, not giving me a chance to escape my destiny. I had to take a written and oral exam to prove my proficiency in Spanish. With a passing score on both, I could apply for the Type 29 Certificate that would allow me to become a bilingual teacher. I would have six years to obtain my teaching license. To be honest, I had no interest in teaching! I took care of kids growing up and I was not going to do it for the rest of my life. My mind was made up. Teaching was not for me.

A few weeks later, I was shocked to get my results. I passed! Miguel was so proud of me, but I still had no interest in pursuing a teaching career. I filed the letter away in my drawer and didn't look back.

A GLIMPSE OF THE FUTURE

One day a request came into our office from a school for a presentation about Mexico. Our Education Coordinator, Rafael Mezo, usually attended to these requests but this time he insisted that I go and talk to the class of fourth-grade students. He claimed no one else was available so I reluctantly agreed. I was surprised by my excitement. I put together as much information about Mexico as I could gather. I also decided to bring props, I wasn't going to show up empty-handed and not give them a chance to taste some of Mexico's prized foods! I brought them conchas and hot chocolate. As the day of the presentation approached, I was getting nervous, but more excited than I had ever anticipated.

On the day of the presentation, I got all dressed up, ready to face my audience of fourth-graders at a school in Palatine, Illinois. In case you're wondering—yes I wore a suit. As we drove there, I was practicing in my head, I was so excited I couldn't focus. Thank goodness Rafael came with me. He mysteriously became available at the last minute. I am not sure if it was for support or because he feared I would back out or maybe both.

As I came into the classroom I could feel my heart beating out of my chest. I had to catch my breath as I stood in front of the classroom. I looked at the students—I was smiling ear to ear. What happened next? All I remember is someone who I didn't expect came out and gave a beautiful presentation. The students applauded in delight. They enjoyed their treats and thanked me for coming.

As we drove back, I couldn't stop thinking about how I felt when I was in front of the students. I felt confident and proud of what I was teaching the students. Did I belong in the classroom? Looking back, I think Rafael and Miguel had this planned all along. Did they see in me the talent to be a teacher? After this experience, I bet you think you know what happened next. Well, you are wrong! I was still not ready to make the jump or admit that I might enjoy teaching, besides I was not ready to abandon my dream of becoming an attorney. Even after feeling the rush of being in front of students.

THE FORK IN THE ROAD

A few weeks later, our new office managers arrived and made personnel changes. They moved staff to other areas to maximize efficiency. I asked the new director to place me in an area that utilized my skills, but he declined my request. The next day, I was assigned to a position where my skills were not utilized and instead of challenging me, it would set me back. I was devastated, to say the least. I was not happy, deep inside of me I knew that this was not the place for me. But I needed a job. What was I going to do? Take the LSAT as scheduled? Stay in this job? There I was staring at the fork in the road. If I stayed, I would be miserable. But I was scared and didn't know what to do.

That night, I cried myself to sleep. I hated the thought of going back to work the next day. As I lay in bed with tears running down my cheek and soaking the pillow, I thought about all of the roadblocks in my attempts to go to law school. I wondered if the universe was trying to give me another message. It had already changed my plans twice. Maybe it was leading me on a different path? Was this the brick hitting my head trying to knock some sense into me? Why was I being so stubborn? I was so lost.

TAKE THE FORK IN THE ROAD

On my way home the next day, I glanced up and saw a Mexican bakery. There it was, my answer! Why was I fighting it? Was it the fear of not succeeding or the fear of giving up on a dream? Was being a lawyer really what I wanted to be?

A smile filled my face. I knew where I belonged. The joy and satisfaction I felt in that classroom in Palatine suddenly came back, and all my fears disappeared! I immediately called Miguel. He was not surprised by my call. How did he know? He somehow saw in me something I did not. I will always be grateful for his tenacity and his desire to help others.

I took my vacation the following week and sent out resumes to every school district in Illinois (at least that's what it felt like). I got an interview that same week. I was ready for a new adventure. My lucky stars were on my side; I got a teaching job! I was going to be a third-grade bilingual teacher!

I LISTENED TO THE UNIVERSE

On August 18, 1996, I signed my contract and drove to meet the principal and take a peek at my new classroom. As I walked into the classroom, I felt like I was floating. I pinched myself to make sure this wasn't a dream. There I was in Room 102, and it was all mine. I smelled the air in the room, and touched the board - I couldn't wait to use the chalk to write on it! It was the best feeling in the world! I knew exactly what I was going to do- I was going to be a teacher! I immediately saw the connection of everything that led me to this moment. I would work with the students to build their knowledge. Every day that I went to work as a teacher— you guessed it—I wore a suit!

Twenty-six years later, I am still working for the same school district. During the first eight years, I went back to school to complete a Master's in Teaching and a Master's in Educational

Administration. After teaching for ten years I left the classroom to become the Parent Coordinator for three years. Afterwards, I served as an Assistant Principal for five years and then returned to my current position as Parent Outreach Liaison. In this position, I utilize all of the skills I learned in my previous jobs and as a business major. I love what I do! It gives me great satisfaction to provide educational opportunities for our community. I'm an educator. This is where I belong!

I would not be here if I kept fighting a universe that was leading me on the path that I was supposed to take. As a child, I was always taking care of my family's children, which ironically probably made me not want a career in Education. No one was more surprised about me becoming a teacher than my mom. She said, "Why are you going to become a teacher if you don't like taking care of kids?" I responded, "I didn't like taking care of kids because no one was paying me, I'm getting paid now!"

I giggle when I think about that junior in college who laughed at the thought of being a teacher. So, if it seems that life is knocking you down and setting you back, maybe it's just trying to steer you in the right direction. Open your mind, and embrace that fork in the road! Follow the path that the universe is lighting up for you. Don't be scared. Maybe it's your destiny. While I may have put aside my dream of wearing a suit as an attorney, my new dream of wearing one every day as an educator for my community is more fulfilling than I could have ever imagined.

REFLECTION QUESTIONS

1. Do you believe in destiny?

2. At what point did you adjust your dreams?

3. How do you know if you are on the right career path?

4. Does the fear of failing keep you in the same job or from taking a risk?

5. 5. How long would you stay in a job where you are not maximizing your potential?

BIOGRAPHY

Isabel Ramirez was born in El Platanal, Municipio de Nocupétaro, Michoacán Mexico. She grew up in the south suburbs of Chicago with her two brothers and two sisters. She has twenty-six years of experience in education. During that time she has held positions as a teacher, parent coordinator, and administrator. Isabel is a first-generation college graduate, with a Bachelor's Degree in International Business from St. Xavier University. She earned a Master of Arts in Teaching from Columbia College and a Master of Arts in Educational Leadership from Lewis University. Isabel is currently the Parent Outreach Liaison for Cicero School District 99. In this position, she collaborates with all of the stakeholders to raise the academic achievement of students. Isabel enjoys baking, cooking, and reading in her spare time.

Isabel Ramirez
jjems2006@outlook.com
Instagram: @iramirez94

Monica Rivers

"There is a difference between knowing you have worth and knowing your worth."

This is the story of a dream coming true. This is the story of freedom from lifelong captivity—a story of pain, self-denial, personal devastation, and the unexpected blessings that came from them—the beauty born from the ashes.

This is a love story: my own love story.

At its core is one radical notion: I am valuable. And not just for my function, role, or relation to others. I hold value in and of myself—nothing added, nothing taken away.

I spent my life denying my inherent value. Building my worth on someone else's opinion of me drove me to please others at any cost. There is a difference between knowing you have worth and *knowing your worth*. And it doesn't just show up in how we feel when we look in the mirror. What we believe about ourselves affects how we live our lives, who we allow to influence us, and even how we love others.

In 2021, I finally discovered the difference.

WHERE IT ALL STARTED

In the earliest years of my life, I began hearing whispers talking down to me and making me feel "less than"—a quiet but persistent insistence that I didn't belong.

I was a little girl in a house of five—two parents, two brothers, and me. My parents loved us and took care of us the best way they knew how. They came from families whose love language was to look out for you—to make sure you were clothed, fed, and healthy—without much warmth or affection. They gave us what they had from their childhood.

I desperately longed to belong at school. I tried to fit in and make friends but faced constant rejection. Once, a group of kids even stole my journal and laughed as they mocked my innermost thoughts.

I felt like no one wanted me.

But still, there was something inside me that longed to be genuine. I have been an entrepreneur even since those early days. Everywhere I looked, even in poverty, I saw possibilities everywhere.

When I was about eight, one of the popular girls began to reach out to me. Our friendship didn't last long, but it did give me a great gift. Her family had a bakery with an abandoned storefront next to it. It looked like it was begging me to bring it to life. I asked my friend, "Why don't we put it to use?" So, we cleaned it up and started telling kids from the school we had a roller-skating rink—one peso for a ride. Before long, so many kids were gliding and twirling around that tiny storefront.

When I saw them enjoying themselves and the business we had created, I discovered something in me I had never seen before: a glimmer of real self-worth. I felt valuable—for my ideas, vision, and who I was. Though I had only known rejection, I saw hope for the future.

DON'T SPEND YOUR LIFE TRYING TO BE SOMETHING YOU AREN'T!

I was only twelve when the whispers had turned into loud declarations. I couldn't bear to go through another day of rejection.

One day, I told my mom, "I don't want to go to school anymore."

"That's fine," she told me, "You don't have to go to school anymore. But if you're not in school, you need to get a job." So, I began my working life at only twelve years old. I spent some time working at a local shoe store, then behind the cash register at a grocery shop, and even worked as a secretary. I learned what adult life was like at these low-paying jobs: hard, tedious work, and abuse. At fifteen, I decided I could only get a better job if I became a completely different person—if I escaped the real me and pretended to be someone else.

My mom had signed me up for a Microsoft Office course, so I thought I knew everything there was to know about computers and applied for a local IT position. (I had no doubt this made me capable of the job...what was I thinking?) I told them I was twenty-one. After some back and forth, they hired me. I wasn't just the "lowly" shopfront girl for nearly two years. I felt like I was finally someone. They trained me so well that not only could I do the job, but I could do it well. I also connected with the company's marketing director and his team. I saw how they promoted the company with third-party hostess agencies and thought, "I could do that!" And at only fifteen, I started an agency managing dozens of models and hostesses. I felt powerful and valuable between my job and my bustling business like I was on top of the world.

But it did not last.

I had taken on more responsibility than my maturity could maintain. I was running away from myself, and the faster I tried to run, the further in over my head I got. Because of my bad decisions, I lost my business and my job.

SETBACKS IN THE JOURNEY

Not long after that, I became pregnant.

My son's birth was one of the best days of my life. But even on that most special day, I couldn't escape falling short. They refused to allow me to leave the hospital until I paid the bill or agreed to leave my baby there.

The disparaging declarations in my mind had risen to thunderous roars. I was still more or less a kid myself, becoming a mother at only eighteen years old. I had been masquerading as an adult for years, but behind that façade, I was still just a little girl craving love or approval.

I desperately searched for love, but every love ended in pain and abuse.

So, in May 2004, I packed my bags, hoping to start a completely new story in a new country. With my two-year-old baby in my arms, I decided to cross the border to the United States. I never imagined what awaited me as an undocumented immigrant across the border.

Accepting to separate from my son in the process was the wrong choice. I was arrested and locked up as a criminal in my attempt, then a few days later, I saw myself again on the other side of the border, begging God to give me back my son. He did, but the dream was still big, so I decided to try again. I thought I had reached my destination when I crossed, but I had not.

In a short time, love came...and with it, domestic abuse, physical blows, and abuse of all kinds. It no longer resembled that great American dream that I imagined, but I felt that there was something more to be done. That whole nightmare—repeating over and over with different relationships, reinforcing my low self-worth—I had no idea how to get out of it and start over until I finally hit rock bottom.

One year later, I was walking in the mall when I approached a kiosk and asked about the price of some earrings. They were so beautiful..."Miss! What price are these earrings?"

"Twenty-five dollars," she replied. My jaw dropped when I heard her answer, and my mind kept thinking about Mexican pesos!

Before going to sleep, my mind was spinning, thinking about the twenty-five-dollar earrings. The following day, I went right to that kiosk in the mall. After taking another look at the merchandise, I figured out how I could make my jewelry. Within a few days, I was making earrings, and again, a new business had started!

It all seemed so simple—long days making earrings, and there I was, ready to go and conquer the world. It was not easy at first, but I decided not to give up, despite the countless setbacks, discouragements, and impossibilities. On one side, I was fighting for success, but I lived with all kinds of atrocities at home.

Thirteen years later, I looked in the mirror and saw the reflection of a nationally renowned businesswoman; I remember telling myself, "It was worth all the pain."

Sometimes, the smallest beginnings produce the brightest adventures. And the most straightforward questions like, "how much are these earrings?" provide us with the most impressive inspiration for our hopes and dreams. Who would have imagined I'd go from selling jewelry on the corner to maintaining a national brand store on those corners? Where you start will not determine where you end. But if you never start, you're already finished.

But even as I gained financial independence, my self-image remained tied to others. I repeated the cycle, trading away pieces of myself to please others because I was holding onto that dream and running away from the idea that I was valuable on my own.

ILLUSIONS AND OLD PATTERNS UNRAVELED

I finally thought I had found true love: my husband.

He didn't hit me; he didn't yell (a lot). He had a career that aspired to make the world a better place. I knew I had finally found the man who would make my dream come true—the prince who would rescue me from my life of sadness. He married me, adopted my son, and we became a family. Unfortunately, it was not as perfect as I had imagined. Instead, he manipulated me. But it wasn't loud, and it wasn't a fist, so I ignored it. I did whatever I needed to do to keep him pleased. I became the perfect dutiful wife, getting made up and making meals and idolizing him.

Deep down, I knew the past patterns were still playing out—the same narcissism and gaslighting—but I let it happen to keep my "dream" alive. I was happy because I finally had my God. And I got so wrapped up in him that I forgot who I was.

And then, without warning, he was gone, just like that.

He had kissed me goodbye when I left for work that afternoon. I didn't know he planned to leave until I came home and found he'd left with half of his things.

The illusion tumbled down on top of me in one fell swoop. Crushed under the weight of his absence, he left me one final taunt: a gun on my dresser, loaded and ready to fire. I genuinely want to believe that he forgot it while preparing to run.

For a moment, it even crossed my mind to do it. After all, what are you left with when your God abandons you?

I spent the next six months in bed, rediscovering depression. I visited counselors; I took depression medication. I felt discarded. Stranded. Hopelessly dejected. And completely unnecessary.

There was a time when I was desperate to create security for my son. That drive kept me going even if things seemed like they couldn't get any worse. But I had long since built a business that kept him cared for—and besides, he was grown and didn't need me like he used to.

I felt truly and completely alone.

In that moment of deepest darkness, I realized I was not alone. I was by myself. In all that time by myself, I saw that I was the only constant in my life. I was the only one who could ever be with me all the time. I had spent my life *fighting* that girl in the mirror. Instead of learning to encourage her, comfort her, and be her friend, I ran from her. I finally saw that I had no choice but to be anyone but her, so I may as well love her.

If I were going to stand by myself, I would stand *for* myself.

I began gathering new evidence for my new identity. Today I chose to live by my declarations...I decided I would no longer vote for rejection and low self-esteem. I would vote for myself by focusing on what I feel, want, and accomplish. I decided I would live by expressing my power and keeping on the journey of rediscovering myself again.

And it's at that moment when you finally remember what version you are, who you are, what you can bring to the table, and what your true value is...everything changes.

You free yourself from the lie that you are not enough. You stop indulging and begin to regain your confidence and power. You start to stay in your truth without caring about the thoughts and opinions of people who should have zero input...because they are not invested in your results.

In my desire to give my son a better life, I had long since built a successful business. But once I began seeing myself differently, I found a new appreciation for that.

It wasn't only something I did for my son; it meant something to me. More than just keeping us safe, it meant that I was capable and savvy. It reminded me of when I had nothing and created something from that nothing.

I began taking classes on things that had always fascinated me. I started traveling to every corner of the US, taking in as much as I could—food, live shows, scenic views, the works.

I ran races, hiked mountaintops, bought dresses, and ate whatever I wanted.

I cultivated friendships with people who wanted nothing from me but my time and company. They loved me for me... and my new understanding of my worth helped me love them better. My pain allowed me to meet the people I needed to so I could live the life I wanted to.

And I created that life, with not one thing in it that I didn't put there.

I fell in love...with life...with me.

All you need is one win at a time, and I guarantee it adds up. Every day, we have the decision to fight the battle we want to fight. The question is, which battle do you want to choose today? The one that will keep you stuck for another day or the one that takes you in the direction you want to go. The best gift that life can offer us is the power of decision. I choose today—and you?

There are days that I still feel like that little girl hiding from the murmurs in the back of her mind. Many women hide from their own discouraging whispers. Don't wear disguises, and don't trade anything for your authenticity. You are your only constant companion, so only you can be your champion.

REFLECTION QUESTIONS

1. What are some of the things you value about yourself?

2. Is there anyone you need to step away from that diminishes your worth?

3. What do you need to do to live your purpose?

BIOGRAPHY

Monica Rivers, born in the state of Sonora, Mexico, has had an entrepreneurial mindset since the age of 9. Beginning her entrepreneurial world at a very young age, she started working at the early age of 12. Her socioeconomic status limited her at that time to continue with her school education. However, that didn't stop her rather motivated her to keep leveling up.

Her journey has taken her from making custom jewelry and selling it on the streets and flea markets to currently becoming a leading entrepreneur with franchises in the Rio Grande Valley in the state of Texas, nationally recognized in the wireless industry, where for more than 15 years she has been recognized with multiple awards, including SBA Young Entrepreneur of the Year by the Rio Grande Valley District office.

Monica currently serves in diverse leadership roles for The John Maxwell Team (now called Maxwell Leadership), the largest Leadership Company on the planet, where she has been certified to coach individuals and groups in the areas of leadership development, professional skills and personal growth.

In 2020, Monica brought to life Latinas Voice, a viable community where the main goal is to help Latina women find their authentic voice. Where the vision is to nurture the transformation of 1,000,000 Latinas around the world to discover their purpose and achieve their goals. Monica has created jobs, opportunities for others, and led teams for years that exhibit great innovation and leadership skills. Her passion is to continue adding value to others to show them that a life of success is not comparable to a life of significance. She believes that if you want to expand and live your dream, know that you can make it happen.

Monica Rivers
monica@latinasvoice.com
facebook.com/MonicaLizbethRivers
https://www.instagram.com/monicalrivers
www.linkedin.com/in/monicalrivers

Andrea Morales

"Your own story could be the guide to salvation for someone else."

Once upon a time in an uncommon place, was the darkest night of my soul; a place where you could have also been; it is located in the middle of the darkness and the solitude where the accumulation of situations overwhelms you, breaks you, overflows, and takes you into a turning point where there are two variables: you either elevate your life, or you go down with it. This was where I was, on my knees in the shower, with a college education just beginning and a baby growing inside me.

This is my story:

I remember being on my knees, praying for direction for what I was about to face. I had seen a slight glimpse of my future crumbling down as if they were sand castles. Something in me told me to say goodbye to the life I had planned for myself to give room for the new life ahead. "I don't know what to do with my life, I don't know what to do with a baby," I cried. I could see my tears dissolve with the shower water. Crying, I begged God to give me a sense of direction, "God, tell me what to do but give me an exact word so that I don't doubt it."

"Continue." This was the response I had heard in my head, so I calmed myself and continued with peace of mind for the rest of that dark night.

The statistics aren't favorable. Thirty percent of young Latin Americans are single moms, according to the data from the United Nations Economic Commission for Latin America and the Caribbean.

I was another number to add to the statistics but even though the situation was adverse, there was something in me that knew that not everything was lost and that there was something more. It felt as if I still had a spark in me that had not gone out to which my own curiosity fanned it more. I decided to take a pen and write my own story, provided with that innate capacity that lies in the feminine to rise from the ashes like a phoenix.

There is an additional power in maternity that we share as women that we are portals to bliss. I named her Constanza Regina; the one who has become my rudder, my anchor, and my sails on Earth, and she now calls me mom.

THE PROTAGONIST OF MY STORY

In my personal journey, I realized that taking my own steps is important before trying to forgive someone. There's a sense of satisfaction that derives from recognizing that I have gone through life with my heart first. My transformation had truly begun the day that I decided to be responsible for myself; I stopped blaming others. My excuses to justify my faults began to disappear and I learned to listen without judging. I gave more attention to my needs and said, "No" to anything that didn't support me without any remorse. I stopped waiting for third party acknowledgements, avoided worry, and focused on finding solutions. I realized that I controlled my own emotions and opted for a healthier diet. I put myself first, learning to organize my own routine and time and decided to work in a way that aligned with my goals. I knew that there would be situations that I couldn't control and that I couldn't force change in them.

I also recognized the value of the things that truly matter. I reconciled with my past, accepting it with gratitude, stopped expecting immediate compensation, and started to put love in everything. I learned to value my friends and family who were around me more and started a better relationship with myself, letting me see life in a different way than before.

The day that I decided to be responsible for myself, I found my own treasure.

I knew then that, "The time in my process was directly proportional to my level of resistance." I understood that my environment, the situations and the people, have been the simplest way of taking responsibility for my existence and not preventing myself from any happiness and becoming the protagonist of my own story.

HAPPINESS IS A PERSONAL RECIPE

I could have chosen not to be responsible for myself and blame anything and everything, but I decided to stop playing the victim card.

I needed to realize what I wanted in my life for it to improve, with the idea of joining all of those components that make me human. It felt like it was the start of a search that would last forever.

I validated what many authors say about happiness, that being happy isn't a mood but instead a decision. So, with all of my might, I vowed to myself to carry forward my best project: my reconstruction as a human being, helped by what motivates me, excites me, my dreams, and my passions. This is my recipe and the compass that locates me in my own north.

Of course, my happiness has a mix of ingredients. When I was thirty-one years old, I tasted failure, which I have taken as an opportunity to make better every time. I added my motives and purpose to my recipe. This recipe doesn't include hate, nor jealousy because of their bitter taste. It includes self-awareness because that is the true empowerment, as well as self-acceptance, which improves my self-esteem. It contains an equilibrium alongside reason, emotion, and action to give it consistency. My recipe also includes dreams, learning, lots of gratitude, inspiration, love, and respect for life, with determination and finally, a whole ton of daring to improve the taste of my life.

In the journey to my happiness, I came across books, courses, mentors, and teachers and my tribes, support networks, and divine connections that have helped me be the woman that I am today. I am also thankful to my parents, who are my pillars in the ground, the love that my mother has given me, especially through the cards and words she would give me during my childhood of how much I meant to her, "You are strong, brave, and capable."

In retrospect I conclude that life, my parents, God and absolutely no one owes me anything, that certainty has given me personal peace.

WHEN YOU LOVE, YOU DON'T LOSE, YOU ALWAYS WIN

Life has led me to become a woman committed to the development and growth of other women, helping to materialize their dreams. In my profession as an independent accountant, I have become a recipient of multiple information. I am focused on being a solver and providing timely data for decision making, not only for my clients, but also for my society. During the pandemic, I decided to contribute voluntarily with time and experience to the development of micro, small, and medium enterprises with the aim of strengthening the family economy of my community and promoting local consumption.

2021 led me to raise my voice within feminism, women's empowerment, the search for gender equality, the protection of sectors of the population, and the protection of women's rights.

In a meeting, I received the proposal of candidacy and felt the weight of a great responsibility. Again, I made an emergency call to God.

"Where do you want to take me with this, why me? Government politics is a corrupt field." The answer in an audible voice in my mind was, "Didn't you say in your prayers that I make you what I want you to be?" The message was clear.

Thus began my political career for the local deputy of District

5, which includes the municipalities of Mascota, San Sebastián, Talpa de Allende, Atenguillo, Guachinango, Mixtlán, Cabo Corrientes, Tomatlán and the municipality of my hometown Puerto Vallarta. The female candidacy was the result of the application of the gender parity law, stipulated in the legislation to ensure equal participation in Mexico's elections. In the shortest campaign period in the history of this country, the largest vote in history took place, where citizens went to the polls wearing masks, respecting a healthy distance and exercising their right to elect 21,368 political representatives. The results were not favorable, but I obtained an undeniable learning and a formation in my character; I still think that he who loves does not fail, but always wins. I signed the pact for sorority, I signed environmental care pacts, and I signed the pact for pro-life and pro-family legislation; with the goal of #QUELOBUENOSEAPARATODOS (may there be good for all).

My participation in the candidacy was in honor of the fighters for labor rights, the suffragettes and all women who have promoted social justice, also to the Association of Professionals and Technicians. The Association planted my political ideals in round tables I attended with my family at six years old, and where I listened indirectly among friends who exposed aspirations and desires to bring welfare to the community of San Juan de Abajo and the young municipality of Bahia de Banderas. My participation was also in gratitude to those who paved the way and in response to my desire to contribute to the people. Love is my flag.

YOU ARE NOT ALONE. GOD IS WITH YOU

A professor once responded to my question, "How did you achieve your professional success? She answered: "There is always an opportunity waiting for you."

In a café, a friend told me, "At this moment we are talking, there are millions of things happening in the world, births, deaths. Your life can change at any moment, but there is something that remains, that is your essence." That afternoon I learned the basis of my identity.

There are always divine connections. God is real and manifests through situations and people, but my eyes had to be trained to see the blessings.

In my life, I have chosen to discipline myself, to have self-control, to learn every day, to be grateful for everything and to champion a purpose to be a spokesperson in conveying a message of goodness and hope, to continually work on maintaining my integrity by balancing all areas of my life.

My growth, my self-discovery, my daughter's guidance and these lines are the personal contributions I make in a loving way with my experiences put at the service of someone else. I enjoy every stage of my life; I am sure I will have many stories to share with my grandchildren in the future.

That dark night of my soul was the catalyst to go upward and make my personal story a guide to salvation for someone else: my descendants, colleagues, sisters, friends.

MY "TO DO" LIST

1. I don't leave home without having more than one reason for feeling happy.
2. I write down my dreams, sensations, quotes, emotions, phrases, and thoughts.
3. I have made a list of people who bring me energy and with whom my energy rises.
4. I have made a commitment to seek my satisfaction by resuming my relationship with myself.
5. I have resumed sending messages of gratitude and good wishes.
6. I have taken time to take a deep breath and exhale a smile in front of the mirror.
7. I have set goals with a date and work one step at a time.
8. I have stopped expecting from others, and have taken my position to contribute, this is my life, no one cares more than me.
9. I have understood the meaning of being a pilot in command.
10. I have set out to develop new skills.
11. I have allowed myself to recognize and validate my intensity and passions.
12. I have returned to gratitude and appreciation for the nature of my environment.
13. I have renewed my peace with myself.

REFLECTION QUESTIONS

1. What lessons have the unexpected turns in your life taught you?

2. How does God communicate with you and you with Him?

3. What ingredients are in the recipe for your happiness?

4. What is your personal contribution to the world?

BIOGRAPHY

Andrea Celina Morales González was born in Puerto Vallarta, Jalisco. She is the oldest of two sisters. She studied public accounting at UNIVA Campus Vallarta, is a business trainer, and CEO of Alpha Integral Consulting. She has been a creator and blogger of freestyle content since 2018. Andrea currently develops altruistic works and is the co-founder of community kitchens in the city of Puerto Vallarta where she mainly helps the homeless and people suffering from addiction. She is a volunteer at Foundation for a Drug Free World and an ambassador of the campaign "The truth about drugs" promoted by Red11s Jalisco. She likes living near the beach, traveling, reading, and is passionate about serving in the ministries of her church while sharing how much God has done with her life.

Andrea Morales
andiemorales.am@gmail.com
Instagram: @andre_acmg

WHAT IS GIVEN FROM THE HEART, IS MULTIPLIED

María del Carmen Ibarra Zepeda

"The genuine love of service fills your soul, your heart and your life with satisfaction."

My family and I were living in Ensenada, Baja California, when suddenly my paternal grandfather got sick. Because of this unexpected news, my dad decided to take us to visit him in San Juan Bautista, Nayarit, where my grandfather lived. Because his health got worse, my mom had to stay and take care of him since my grandfather lived alone and had no one to take care of him. My dad left us there and went to look for work outside this area, since there was not much opportunity for him there. However, a lot of time went by without him being able to come back to see us, since he found a job as far as Puerto Vallarta. He was quite far away and because of that we went through some nights of hunger, lacking, and in general had a lot of needs.

WORKING AND LEARNING

I remember that in that place the movie theaters were

in tents. The town was a little far from the city and there was only one *corrida*—that's what they called the bus. There was one departure in the morning and one in the afternoon for the return trip. One day I begged my mom to take us to see the movie they were showing that afternoon and my mom, sadly and with tears in her eyes told me, "We don't have money *hija,* not even for a tortilla." But with a lot of confidence, she also told me, "But we are not going to stay here, I promise you! You have to get an education to get ahead." After that, my little sister and I sat by the door to listen to the movie from afar. From a distance we could hear a little because they were playing a loudspeaker.

Other profound moments for me were when my mother would send me to neighboring houses to sell the sewing napkins she would weave. Sometimes it was *duritos,* or tamales, or whatever she could prepare. My mother has always been a warrior and has persevered since we were in great need. In addition to that, I loved to help her and make her feel my support. With those experiences, I realized that I liked sales and dealing with people. When I got a little older, I would go to a godmother's house to help her with the housework. She gave me a weekly allowance, which allowed me to help buy food for my family, or for school expenses. We had many siblings at home and it was imperative to support them.

When my dad came to see us, I remember he used to make my sister Marichuy and I dance on the edge of the fence of the house, and when we danced, we had a great show of children and my dad was fascinated with us! He loved dancing with us and to this day he still loves it. My dad is also very creative and talented. My dad, also a songwriter, has over 100 songs recorded. When I was in high school, something he used to do a lot was write rough drafts of songs and give them to me so I could type them out for him. I got a thrill out of it and I admired his talent so much! He still has a guitar and a suit that the singer Cornelio Reyna gave him as a gift.

NEW OPPORTUNITIES IN PUERTO VALLARTA

Very sporadically, uncles from Ensenada or Puerto Vallarta would visit us and bring us groceries, gifts, and of course we were grateful and happy. During one of my uncles' visits, my mother had already talked to my father and convinced him that I should go with my uncles to study in Puerto Vallarta. We all came together with my uncles so that I could move and stay to study. My dad was actually living in Puerto Vallarta and had a job as a chauffeur; however, they took me to live with his brother—my uncle Juan who had just gotten married. We lived in Olas Altas, a very beautiful and touristic area.

Once the euphoria of arriving in Puerto Vallarta was over and when my mother and siblings returned to the ranch, I cried every afternoon and every night. I missed them and felt a great emptiness in my heart. It was very difficult to be without them all that time, but I was comforted knowing that one day I would be able to have a good job and help my parents and siblings get ahead. Thank God, I did.

My father enrolled me in a private school, *Instituto*

Comercial Vallartense, and there I did my studies and finished my accounting degree. My daddy did everything possible and impossible to support me with the tuition. My uncle Juan was a great motivator for me to choose that career since he is also an accountant and I used to see him wearing a very elegant suit and an executive briefcase. I imagined someday I would be able to do it too. When I was studying accounting, I started a job working in the afternoons. Those were heavy days since I would leave work at 9:00pm. At that time, I would start doing my homework for school, to be ready for the next day at 7:00am. Sometimes I would fall asleep without finishing my homework because I was so tired, but I always made the effort to complete everything. After a few years my uncle Juan moved and we changed houses. We stayed there for a little while, but then I was sent to live with another relative, my great-aunt Margarita. Her family had a grocery store and I agreed to learn and take care of it and to cover it at times.

Eventually my dad brought my mom and siblings and we all went to live with another uncle for a while. However, it was not a very good experience since there were many of us—7 children and my parents, a total of 9 people. In a short time, we moved to a small room in the Lopez Mateos neighborhood. At that time a beautiful aunt named Isidra bought a taco cart in order to give my mother a job—a beautiful gesture I will always be grateful for. My mother worked at night and I took care of my siblings. We all longed for her return because my aunt always sent us taquitos, which for our humble appetite was a delicacy.

I was always studying in the mornings and working in the

afternoons to help with my school expenses and as much as possible for the home. Several of my jobs included a stationery store, a lawyer's office, and an accounting internship at the Hotel Posada Rio Cuale. The beautiful ambient music at that hotel is something I remember clearly and since then I have loved all instrumental and opera music.

AN EXEMPLARY MOTHER

As I mentioned before, my mother is a warrior, persevering, talented and restless, worthy of admiration. When she was in Vallarta, she also had several jobs like me. Not to mention, she embroiders and knits beautifully! She managed to study Dressmaking at the DIF (System for the Integral Development of the Family). By the way, when we were at my grandfather's ranch, she also studied by correspondence to become a nurse and was a volunteer at the village clinic. I was her guinea pig because she would practice the injections with me—she would tell me it was vitamins and that it would help me grow...from her I inherited my restlessness.

I believe that she also decided to study nursing because of the death of my little brother. He died when he was 3 months old due to the lack of medical services and money to take care of him. They did everything they could. My mother did not stop crying for a long time and it broke my heart. On another occasion, my brother Pablo was bitten by a spider on his knee while we were all kneeling together praying the Rosary. He became very serious, his voice trembled, and he literally said goodbye to us, but blessed God he was saved.

Similarly, on one occasion at home, my mother was bitten by a scorpion when she was splitting a log and she became very ill. We took her to the clinic and the doctor asked me to bring her some hot cinnamon. I prepared it for her in a pot where she used to put the butter, but I didn't realize and I brought it to her like that! My mother saw me, stroked my head, said nothing and drank it just like that. Always so much love from my dear mother!

A PATH OF DEVELOPMENT AND STRUGGLE

The day of my graduation arrived and I immediately decided to look for a professional job. With all the pressure that perhaps necessity gave me and with a recommendation from my teacher Aaron who taught me accounting, I was hired at a small hotel next to the Sheraton. I was super happy! But God had other plans for me. I had made a commitment before I started working to cover a vacation for a cousin who was getting married and going away on her honeymoon. She worked at the Costa Vida Vallarta Hotel. I kep my commitment and almost immediately, they offered me a job with the option to stay there or work at another hotel that the same company was about to open, La Jolla de Mismaloya.

La Jolla de Mismaloya was a beautiful, magical place where I met important people in my life. They were generous in teaching us, giving us support and motivated me to always be prepared and continue to develop myself. I was always there, willing to help no matter if it was in maintenance, cooking, housekeeping, etc. I learned from everyone. A wonderful mentor—Mr. Santiago

Gutiérrez Haces—an incredible human being, brilliant, talented, with a strong character but a great teacher, made that hotel shine. Along with him, he developed us, his team, in a professional manner. He turned the hotel into a *The Leading Hotels of the World,* a prestigious title, and we became ISO 9000 certified, and received a variety of other awards. It was a great learning experience working with him and his entire management and operations team.

During my stay in La Jolla de Mismaloya, I was still starting out and there was still a need at home. We were already 8 children and my dad was still working as a cab driver. It wasn't enough to support all the needs of the family so while working I jumped into product sales and sold almost everything. In a couple of seasons, I sold toys and I remember being in the public bus carrying tricycles, children's bicycles, etc, but I was not ashamed. I was very pretty in heels, well-groomed and armed with my load of toys making the necessary effort. There was always someone who helped me, thank God, to carry my bags that I carried with me, and even the cab drivers of the hotel site, if they saw me, they gave me a ride. What a blessing.

As time went by, with a lot of effort my father bought a lot and we had to build our own house, since we lived in a rented room. So, on my own initiative, I began to hold raffles to continue contributing to my family. I made an effort and went wherever it was necessary to sell raffle tickets. There was an area of construction personnel in the hotel and in my lunch break I would go there to sell them. Blessed God, everyone always supported me both at the hotel and with their acquaintances. I think they realized the effort I was putting into everything and saw me do it in a brave and dignified way.

A BRIGHT FUTURE OF SERVICE

As I mentioned before, I am very restless and I love to develop myself and learn new things or improve what I know. So even when working I have always kept on taking courses, seminars, workshops, etc. Everything I could regardless of the subject. In the integration activities at the Hotel La Jolla de Mismaloya, in a hotel competition I participated and was crowned as Miss Congeniality. It was so much fun to live that experience! Also, there I met my now husband, Jose Luis, and father of my 2 precious sons, Aldair and Gibran. But that's another story!

On several occasions I had the opportunity to be offered jobs from other places. However, I had no interest in moving, as I was very happy in that hotel; until the hotel was sold to another hotel chain. I was still working for them when 3 different companies curiously at the same time offered me a job right in this transition. No doubt God has his own ways of manifesting himself. I entrusted myself to him and chose Tukari Travel Agency, in a new challenge as Administrative Manager. I was excited and so happy. When I was interviewed by the owner—a beautiful lady with an impressive charisma and a genuine love for tourism service Norma Furlong—I knew I had found another great mentor. She continued to instill in me a love of service and the importance of promoting Destination Tourism. I also remember her telling me, "While you are here, please never miss any important event of your children." Those were magic words for me to decide to stay in that place, because I felt the care and support. Of course, there were also challenges and difficult times, but with perseverance, dedication and responsibility, I was able to move forward with my work commitment and carry out my home responsibilities as a mother in a balanced way.

Without a doubt, the genuine love of service fills your soul, your heart and your life with satisfaction. It makes you want to follow the chain of helping others, as you can always give that extra! Service is the best way to be grateful, to transcend and to enrich your life and the life around you. For me, it is important to know that it has been worth everything I have gone through to be where I am right now, to see my family with me, healthy and happy. To enjoy with them the fruit of my work, of my effort and of my genuine love in doing it; to wish to leave a legacy of doing things with authentic love.

I am convinced that everything in life has a reason for being, that God is not wrong; that without those difficult things that we all went through, we would not be the human beings we are now! I am very grateful to God for my life, my children, my husband, my family, my friends and the wonderful people and things he has given me. I send blessings to all of them, especially my parents, my siblings and everyone who intervened in my life, so that I may be the happy and blessed woman that I am!

REFLECTION QUESTIONS

1. Have you had experiences that have shaped you into the person you are now?

2. What are you passionate about and how can you develop it further?

3. Is service and support to others important to you?

BIOGRAPHY

María del Carmen Ibarra Zepeda is a woman with many talents, and who always sees the positive side of everything. She is a woman infinitely grateful to God for the wonderful people He has sent into her life. Carmen is the mother of her sons Luis Aldair and Gibran Josué, and wife of José Luis, and is very proud and grateful to have such a beautiful family! Carmen works in the Tourism Industry in a beautiful, divine and blessed hotel, with wonderful owners with a noble and generous heart. She has her degree and studies in Accounting. She is founder and president of the Club Vallartense de Mujeres Ejecutivas y Empresarias de PVR, providing courses and workshops for personal growth and altruism activities, since 2004.

Carmen has participated and taken several courses and seminars including: The Administrative Manager in Modern Business, Executive Woman, Leadership and Effective Communication, Distinctive H, Public Relations, Speaking Skills, Writing Skills, Competency Based Executive Training, Total Quality, Human Relations, Rules of Etiquette, Customer Service, Quality Control, Time Management, Management Skills Development, The 7 Habits of Highly Effective People and more. Carmen is also the Coordinator of the Readers Group in her Parish.

María Del Carmen Ibarra Zepeda
cibarraz@hotmail.com
Instagram: carmen.ibarra.zepeda

INTERNAL PEACE: THE GREATEST GIFT YOU CAN GIVE YOURSELF AND OTHERS

Cristina Flores

"God is the only one that gives us internal peace."

Part of living life is having to face obstacles, but how much you let them affect you is what matters.

My story begins in Mexico. I am the youngest girl of six siblings; four brothers and one sister. My siblings and I grew up in a difficult environment, but also as children we played a lot with all the neighbors in the street. Roller skating, go karts, bicycles, hide and seek, we had a lot of fun. My father was very strict with us but my mother always gave him the benefit of the doubt. We would often get yelled at and sometimes my brothers would get hit, that was how they were educated back then. As I grew older we were very busy because my mom always made us do something. We joined a swimming team and would practice from 4:00 pm until 10:00 pm everyday after school. We became a part of a national synchronized swimming team. We lived in a rich neighborhood, even though we were not, which helped us to cultivate good relationships, school scholarships, and also made us eager to learn and improve ourselves. We were friends with all of the wealthy families so we got the chance to enjoy whatever they had too. It was nice because we gave them our friendship and company.

GROWING UP

My father didn't finish elementary school, so he didn't have much of an education. He tried to do whatever he could to help my mom, but I remember her saying he helped her when we were young but not when we grew up. My mom came from a well-off family but fell in love with my dad and it was difficult for her to defend us. My mom adored my father and what he said would go. Her mom told her if you marry him you won't have any money. Yet, she worked hard so that she could buy not only one but two houses. My mom always worked so hard. was the only sister that never got anything from her parents. My grandfather was a lawyer and my grandmother didn't work, though she was very smart and spoke many languages. All of my siblings left the house at a young age. They didn't have a good relationship with my father but as they grew older, they grew closer to him.

My mom was a dancer and acted with famous Mexican stars, like Pedro Infante, but she left everything to marry my dad and become a dance teacher. She made a studio at home and would teach all day long. She had to support the family, leaving my older sister, Carmen, with the responsibility of caring for me. It wasn't easy for her to do this; she should have been worrying about other things at her age but I felt protected because of her. I am grateful for the many years that she took care of me. Even now, she is great at taking care of her family and she is very involved with her children and her grandchild, that's the way she is. I used to come to her house with my daughters every year in the States because I was very close to her.

My father was never home since he was always busy selling goods and working for a dentist. I remember him doing so many things and he loved to sell. I love to sell too, maybe I got it from him. He was even a bullfighting helper at one point. Gambling was his number one hobby, he lost a lot of money, and hardly ever won. We had a lot of art in the family as both of my parents painted in their free time and my brothers were musicians. Like I said, my mom kept us busy all the time. It was because of her that I ended up competing in swimming in many places: the United States, Canada, Central America. My sister even reached the Olympic level and competed in Japan, Argentina, and other places. I remember my mom was so healthy. She always told me that working out was the solution to everything. We hardly got sick, but if I had a headache she would say "Go swimming you will feel better."

I knew that my mom wanted to take care of us, but she felt overwhelmed with having to keep up with her job and having to care for us since she was the money maker. She began with her studio at home but soon was able to create a big dance studio called Danza FLORES Studio. She also organized festivals in big theaters. She was truly the breadwinner of the family. I think I got my ambition to work hard from my mother. She fought to give us the best life she could, even if that meant her having to work extremely hard.

Thankfully, learning English was the least of my concerns. Since I have always loved to speak it, it came naturally. I remember always singing in English when I was little, even though I never knew if I was actually speaking the right words. I was in private and public schools and it helped my learning a lot but I also got a lot of help from my neighbor, Mrs. Chela Limon, who was very well-off. More than that, she was a very nice human being. She was my godmother, sort of speaking, and she helped through many things. She owned a private school and was an English teacher. Even though she was married she was lonely, so I used to sleep at her house to keep her company. She helped me with a scholarship to become a bilingual executive secretary and I was even able to buy my second car that had belonged to her. She was very nice to me and I was always responsible and paid my debts.

Eventually I decided to go to the USA, all of my brothers had left and I didn't want to be alone in Mexico so I followed them. My parents gave me their blessing and with my money from working as a bilingual executive secretary at the bank of Mexico, PepsiCo Inc. I was able to go. My brother, Luis Antonio, helped me to get into a school of cosmetology. My brother and his wife—my friend, Silvia—helped us a lot.

It was so hard for them to have all of the family living in their house, so then I moved to my sister's house with her husband and children. When I finished school, I worked for 2 years but I realized that I didn't see myself doing it for the rest of my life. I felt alone in the US, even with the company of my brothers. I wanted to live in Mexico. I said I wanted to live the Mexican Dream and open my business in Puerto Vallarta even though I had never been there before.

BEING RESILIENT

I wanted to return to my city in Mexico; it felt like a piece of me was missing. The opportunity to come home came when my sister was getting married. I was excited to see her but more excited to see my hometown. Before leaving, I told my brother that I would leave them my car and money in case I couldn't come back. When I passed through immigration, they noticed that I was working in the US illegally and asked if I would rather be deported or go back on my own, so I happily booked a ticket and flew back home. This was my first blessing in disguise because I didn't have to worry about anything but returning back. With that being said, when I was 26 years old, I was back on familiar soil. I felt at peace again, being around the environment that I grew up in. Later on, I was invited to work in Puerto Vallarta in a timeshare so I packed my bags once again and moved.

I came to Puerto Vallarta in September and I met my ex-husband in a club, which I never wanted to go to, but after a month and a half of dating, I decided to marry him. We formed a beautiful family with three daughters, Estefania, Maria Fernanda, and Renata. What I believed was a fairytale turned out to be the exact opposite. At the beginning I was doing very well and I helped him but he eventually started making more money. After two years of marriage we had our first daughter and I decided to quit and stay home. I was the submissive wife with the triumphant husband. I wasn't happy like this. When I taught him how to sell timeshares, it brought a lot of women and money to him and I reverted back to my younger self—breaking the trend of the woman having to obey her man in order to keep him by her side— I divorced him. I decided that I didn't want that life for my girls. I wanted something better for them and I knew that stepping away would be the best thing I could do for them.

My divorce was difficult. Initially because my mom adored my ex-husband and told me not to leave, but in the end she was the one who helped me. She told him, "You made another family. Leave Cristy alone." So she gave me the courage to get him out of the house which he really did not care about at all. He never cared about his daughters and even told me nobody is going to love you with three children. It was very hard to divorce him but what hurt the most was that my girls didn't have a father to love and be there for them and that he didn't care for them. He didn't see them for two years. He only showed up when I was selling the house because I was starting my own business. I thank God every day that He gave me the strength to raise my family and helped me with my business so that I could send them to a good school. I did as much as I could to give them the best, like many single mothers do.

MY BEAUTIFUL DAUGHTERS

Estefania, my oldest, is very intelligent and beautiful. She was very hurt by the divorce, more than my other girls. She loved her father a lot. They are very much alike, and sometimes I would regret divorcing him because she lost her father. We used to talk a lot but she would outsmart me and I wouldn't understand her sometimes. She currently speaks 3 languages—Japanese, English, and Spanish. She finished her degree in International Relations in Guadalajara and eventually Vallarta was not enough for her. She is living in Japan and doing very well. She became what she wanted to be, a very important and successful Mexican woman in Japan. I do not see her as much as I would like to, but God knows better and I know I will see her soon. I pray and send my love everyday.

Maria Fernanda, my bebesita—*mamacita* she used to call me—wanted to go to Australia and do her residency and do everything she wanted. She was a free spirit and loved every sport in the world, especially surfing. Unfortunately, one day after work she had a car accident and went to heaven. That was and still is the worst thing that ever happened to me. She was so happy, full of life, and loved everyone. Everybody loved her. She used to call me and say "Thank you for everything mom. You are the best." It made me feel so good and made me so happy. She made me so proud! As a mom, we always want what's best for our children but God knew better and an angel. I know she is with me all the time, but I really miss her a lot and sometimes still feel this is a dream and I will see her again. When I went to Australia, an angel helped me through all that, God never leaves us alone. He will send you someone. I feel her and talk to her everyday and I know she takes care of me and helps me to go through this life.

I teach catechism in my church and her ashes are there. I go visit with my children and teach them to pray for all the people to rest in peace. She is in heaven and every week that I go, my children bring her a flower and ask me "Aren't we going to see the little girl?" Children are so beautiful...

Renata, my Reny, my little baby I called her *Solecito*. My little baby is 24 years old now. She is an architectural engineer, working in the town hall happily as can be. She is truly a star, very intelligent and strong. Although she will always be my baby, she really helped me a lot. For a while, she was living in Cancun by herself. Her father never cared for her because he is very narcissistic, so when this tragedy happened, she agreed to come and live here in Vallarta and we have been together ever since 2018. I have to thank her so much for being with me, we have lived through the grief together, which is not easy. I admire her so much because she is very smart. Losing her father and her sisters was not easy, she misses Mariafer a lot. People called them twins and even though she works at the City Hall, she still helps me with the spa as the web master. She is my angel on earth.

KEEPING FAITH AND MOVING FORWARD

My brother, Felipe, has been my partner in Puerto Vallarta for so many years. I started my business in 2009 and he has always helped me. One day he ended up losing his wife due to cancer, it happened in just one year. Then he had an alcohol and drug addiction, diabetes, and hypertension, so we decided to take him to a clinic to help. My family was very close during this time. He has been there 3 times so God keeps me busy. I would often take care of mine and my brother's kids, which was truly a blessing. Between taking care of the 5 children and working, I was always busy. I also began to teach catechism classes and I have been teaching for 20 years now since my divorce which added to the busy schedule.

Even with all of these great blessings, my life has had plenty of difficult moments. One was being diagnosed with Hodgkin's lymphoma, which thankfully, in 2015, went into remission. The biggest tragedy of my life was the loss of my adored Marifer, my happy girl. My mom and her were the ones taking care of me during that time of unwellness. My mom came to live with me because my father passed away. My daughter would come to visit me and got me into juicing and other healthy habits. Even though I went through chemotherapy and lost my hair, I did not care. My girls were with me and my mom too, I had so much love from both of them and now they are my angels in heaven.

When I look back at my life, I remember the difficult moments that I have gone through but instead of looking at them with regret or hatred, I look with gratitude because those are the moments that helped me find peace within myself. I was asked which message I wanted to leave behind. I want people to remember me as a woman who fought to keep shining a little bit of light and love to the lives of others, even in moments of absolute darkness. We must remember to live with happiness and if you are unable to, at least give yourself enough rest to never lose hope. Everyone goes through obstacles at some point in their life, whether they're small bumps that can be hopped in no time, or bigger bumps that take a little longer to get over. What matters is how much you let these obstacles affect you and what you do from that point on. You can either decide to let those obstacles weigh you down and define you or you can take them as lessons to learn and grow from them.

DAYSPA, my business, has always been a blessing to me, although it brought lots of stress. My spa has been around for 23 years and I am blessed to have a bountiful amount of work. I love the people I see every day and find bliss that we are able to give them some rest from their lives that contain many obstacles and hard work. It's beautiful seeing people from opposite economic statuses come in carrying the same amount of stress as everyone else and being able to help them, lift their spirits and give them a moment of rest. The body has memory and it guards wounds and if we don't take the time to relieve some of them, we may never find the peace that we are looking for. My three girls helped me so much in the spa with their technology and even as masseuses, but the most beautiful part is that they chose their own future. They didn't have to go through what I did and they lived their own lives how they wanted to.

In addition, God has always been the one who has been and will always be the best part of my life. Without him, I wouldn't have been able to get through what I have. The absolute and perfect peace you can receive is from God and the Virgin Mary. She is my mother in heaven and she takes care of me and the way she obeys and loves God teaches us how to be happy no matter what. We both cried when we lost our child and I trust and adore him the way she did. God has always been the one who has held me, accompanied me, and has given me the strength and happiness every day to live. Not only that but to help any person who has crossed my path or who He has guided me to.

I remember my mom taught me this: *Who does not live to serve does not serve to live, we need to serve, live, and be happy.* No matter how many obstacles I face in life, I know that God gives and God takes away. I live in peace because God controls my life, I keep my pain in my faith. **Live as if it were the last day of your life!**

REFLECTION QUESTIONS

1. How can you serve others with your talents or time?

2. Do you let God into your life? How has he blessed you in your life?

3. What can you do or who do you have in your corner when you go through a difficulty in your life?

BIOGRAPHY

Cristina Flores is a mother, successful entrepreneur, change-maker, and owner of DAYSPA in Puerto Vallarta, Mexico. She has been in business for over 23 years and continues to dedicate her life of service. Her spa is well known and is a top destination for those who wish to experience peace and relaxation.

Cristina is very involved in her community and shares her talents and time with others. She is a catechism teacher at her local church and prides herself in sharing her faith and deviation to her students. She is also a cancer survivor and thanks her family and God for being by her side.

Cristina loves her hometown of Puerto Vallarta, and enjoys the beautiful sunrises and sunsets that this beautiful place gives her. She believes in a life of service and always doing what's best for others.

Cristina Flores
Instagram:cristy_paz1
www.spapv.com
wcdspa@gmail.con

Dinorah Gómez

"I believe in Love as the most powerful force that never dies out."

MY ROOTS

I grew up with the most beautiful example of love that a couple can give to their children.

Love is the most sublime expression in every sense. My parents, two restless young newlyweds, with no other luggage other than their dreams, arrived in Puerto Vallarta in1962. This was precisely when John Houston, prestigious Hollywood film director, was shooting in this jungle paradise the movie *"The Night of the Iguana"*. Starring in the film were the artists of the moment Eva Gardner and Richard Burton, husband at that time of the also famous actress Elizabeth Taylor who accompanied her consort in the filming of the movie, causing news for the media and tabloids.

Those were times of great progress and the city was growing at an accelerated pace. Puerto Vallarta had become a tourist destination that rose to fame. Overnight, the name of our city appeared in the headlines of many newspapers around the world and in show business. There was construction of highways, airports, hotels, restaurants, bars, and nightclubs here in town. Journalists, politicians, artists, rich and important people from the United States, other parts of Mexico and around the world began to arrive.

At the same time the urban sprawl steadily grew, men and women joined the workforce as bricklayers, carpenters, waiters, waitresses, cooks, plumbers, electricians, small merchants and street vendors, and teachers. Entire families were looking for the opportunity of a better life. All these people soon needed housing and services such as electricity, water, gas, infrastructure, transportation, schools, etc. The accelerated growth overtook the supply and finding housing was almost impossible, as there was none at that time, which made life very hard for all these people.

There was a notorious contrast that showed the inequality between some and others. My father, who already had a background as a student leader and fighter for causes in favor of those who had less, soon understood that he had found a good way to put it into practice and work. He loved to serve and help others. He was always defending the underdog. My mother, always willing, with a generous heart and the whole family, were included in this noble work.

Both my parents were inserted into the social, political, and cultural life of the city. They exercised leadership and worked tirelessly to defend human rights, women's rights, children's rights, the right to education and culture. They also defended the right to housing, work and labor, better salaries and a dignified life. They became social activists and promoters of our culture. Little by little they were also joined by people who wanted to help.

They were a great team!

I remember the days of my childhood and adolescence with much enthusiasm and gratitude. I spent them accompanying my parents in their countless tasks. We constantly visited distant neighborhoods and marginalized areas. It hurt to see so much need of those who had less. We brought a little joy to all of them through what I remember my father used to call "cultural and art festivals for the people". The people welcomed us with pleasure and my father would manage to get support from the hotel businessmen and the union. They would lend him their musical and folkloric dance groups to present to this public, who after all were also people from Puerto Vallarta.

I was the oldest of seven siblings, so naturally I became involved. I started organizing games for the children and I played a little guitar. So, if there was an opportunity I would sing at the events we hosted too. We did everything and helped in any ways we could. Sometimes I had to arrange chairs or hand out water. I also took folkloric dance classes and sometimes I would dance with my group. Oh, how nice it is to remember those special times...

Growing up, I liked to read poetry and recite it. I represented my school in local and state contests on several occasions. It didn't take me long to stand in front of an audience and recite poetry by Amado Nervo, Mario Benedetti, Gustavo Adolfo Bécquer, and many more. We read books and shared stories. It was a beautiful time of so much rich learning.

While I learned lessons in school I learned virtues at home. I learned by example that serving your neighbor is a way of loving! I learned that giving is a principle of life!

I learned that we all need each other collectively! My parents and their love for serving have been my biggest inspiration.

NEW ENDEAVOURS

Although I loved the arts so much and had the opportunity to develop myself in that field since my childhood, when I finished high school, I had to make a decision whether or not to pursue a career in the arts or whether or not I would even pursue a university degree. At that time there were no universities in our city, nor was it common for women to study university careers. If I wanted to continue studying I had to leave my town, take the challenge and achieve what my grandmother and many women of her generation could not. My father—who always supported women and showed great respect for them and their struggle to occupy a better place in the social scheme—made me see how lucky I was to have the moral and economic support of my family. That made me feel strong and confident that I could achieve this endeavor. With my heart full of hope I went to achieve my dream. I enrolled in the Law School of the University of Guadalajara. I graduated five years later as a lawyer and returned to my hometown with a profession that has allowed me to learn about the law in order to serve my community.

Life has been generous to me and I have so much to be grateful for. Currently, my firm and company, with a history of more than 35 years, has been strengthened with ideas and a new vision brought by my eldest daughter, who is also a lawyer and is now my partner.

I feel very proud and fortunate to work together in this new stage of my life. We assist, free of charge, many Civil Associations that work for our community. More than 12 years ago, I started to get involved with the Civil Association that manages the most important cultural entity in the entire Banderas Bay area.

The first library in our city was founded 25 years ago. It's everyone's house. A public, formative, necessary, and vital precinct to reforest thought and transform lives. It's a cultural offering through the arts that manages to counteract the vicissitudes of life and the terrible situation of children and young people who, with no other option, take the wrong path and live today trapped in addictions of all kinds. Some of which are part of the most destructive business of our society...drug trafficking.

In April 2019, I assumed the position of President of the Board of Directors of this institution with a very firm determination to work on projects that help this cause. However, to achieve this I had to face the most difficult challenge I ever imagined; a pandemic!

The whole world was shaken and paralyzed by this news.I remember that many of us thought that it would last fifteen days, that soon the governments of the world would find a solution. Days, weeks, months went by and the pandemic continued and grew, and so did the fear and uncertainty. Our library, which does not receive continuous financial support from any government and lives on the resources provided by donors, began to suffer financially. Businesses closed, commercial activity came to a standstill, thousands of cultural centers and libraries around the world were also forced to close their doors. Cultural life, which provided a respite for many, was greatly affected.

Faced with this Goliath, we had to come up with strategies to deal with it. We did not stand idly by. We joined forces with people who, like us, were also willing to help. We formed a great team and together we put together plans and community projects to overcome the terrifying effects of the pandemic and the measures taken by our governments to force us to stay home. Miraculously, we received the donation of a single person that we remember with much affection and gratitude since this allowed us not to close our doors and to continue operating. It was a winding road, stressful, but beautiful at the same time, because we managed to reach our objectives despite the pandemic. Today we can share this story of coming out stronger with love and faith.

I mention LOVE again, because the help that each and every one of us who participate in this story contributes makes us donors of our time, our abilities, and our willingness to serve.

This is undoubtedly an expression of love and service to others.

REFLECTION QUESTIONS

1. What kind of story would yours be?

2. What will you do to improve not only your life, but the lives of those around you?

3. How has the love and support you have received throughout your life shaped you into who you are now?

BIOGRAPHY

Dinorah Gómez is a lawyer by profession, artist at heart, entrepreneur and cultural promoter.

She has been married for 33 years to the love of her life, and is mother of three daughters and one son. Dinorah considers herself lucky to have such a beautiful and supportive family. She currently holds the position of AD Honorem as President of the Board of Directors of Biblioteca Los Mangos Centro Cultural, Asociación Civil in Puerto Vallarta. The only library that offers cultural services to the city and the entire Banderas Bay area. She is proud to work and represent this library which is the very heart of community cultural life.

Dinorah Gómez
dinorah_gomez01@hotmail.com

THE MAGIC OF RESILIENCE

Amaranta Gaytán

"Today is a great day to be proud of your process, all that you have accomplished and all that you have learned."

Each of us has experienced ups and downs in our lives, regardless of our age, stability or level of success. Occasionally, we are overwhelmed by a sense of emptiness. It is part of our life to have moments of loneliness, sadness, and confusion. However, the human strength that every human being has inside is something so special and important to recognize. We are resilient and capable of overcoming the obstacles that come our way. Helping people realize that inner power is my passion.

I am grateful to be able to tell my story and what fills my heart through these short words. Being able to retell my story begins in April 2022 when, for the first time, I looked back on my early years of life with nostalgia and a strong desire to go back in time. I decided to look through my family album and try to be able to contemplate the memories of those wonderful years together. Those special moments where we cherished the times without cell phones. The scent of those old photos is truly indescribable!

I start sighing, close my eyes and continue remembering. I am excited to feel those moments, the hugs and the energy and warmth of those people, remembering those festive days and every birthday, Christmas and New Year's. I hug with love and show gratitude—one of the most beautiful ways to appreciate our life and maximize our existence. And today, I show appreciation and gratitude for all the moments lived day by day that have made me this wonderful woman of 35 years.

Now I ask myself: How do I begin to recount the moments of inspiration that got me here? Would my story be worth telling?

It only took me a few minutes to decide. I took my pen, a small notebook from the MAGIX meeting, and began to write with my heart. I feel with great passion every beat of my heart!

FOLLOWING MY CURIOSITY

I grew up within the diversity of two family pillars: my mother's Zamora side and my father's Gaytán side. Growing up, my education was composed of a diversity of beliefs, cultures and ideas that my parents instilled in me but that out of curiosity I learned on my own as well.

My two pillars were a mixture of values, dreams and challenges. My parents Graciela Zamora and Humberto Gaytán, represent strength and courage, which both gave me the desire to overcome any obstacle with the most beautiful virtue "humility", without overlooking the unconditional love of my sisters.

I remember the winter of 1992 as if it were yesterday. I was 5 years old when I developed a curiosity about the world, the mind and the subtle way we communicate. A personal event at that age would mark my life. As a result of this event, I grew up with fears and insecurities, limitations and the undeserved mindset. It impacted my adolescence, my youth and later in my adulthood. I knew I thought differently as a 5-year-old typically doesn't fill her head with ideas, of how people are or how they think, but wants to play! Perhaps I already knew within me, the inspiration and the basis of what I was going to dedicate my life to.

I grew up with the dream of being a person who brought empathy, listening, moral support to the world—someone who would help others understand their emotions. Something that was missing for me as I grew growing up and developed. It was then when I was 12 years old that I discovered the world of psychology and philosophy. This is my *IKIGAI*—the Japanese secret to finding life's purpose.

I began my education by reading in school libraries or reading those unpackaged books in public bookstores. That's how my teenage dream came true. By the time I turned 17, I was sitting in the front row of the university studying psychology. I remember attending classes with great excitement, seeing my professors passionate about human behavior and my classmates with that mix of uncertainty and happiness. On the day of my graduation, I knew that my life purpose was materializing, how lucky I felt! That day I knew the satisfaction of achievement and it gave me the motivation to push myself and show that I could still go for more.

The path of psychology is not an easy one, as you gain

knowledge and understand that knowledge really begins with yourself. It forces you to discover your greatest fears, recognize and love your dark side and work with those wounds that had not been healed. It says that if you want different changes, you must start with you. How difficult, isn't it? It was then that I decided to be my own guinea pig and with the guidance of my teachers, I began my personal work. With that came the completion of my studies practicing in the areas of clinical psychology and work psychology, achieving my degree with honors. So yes, I felt ready for the most important school, the school called LIFE. I felt free and light.

THE SPROUT

My personal growth was strengthened by the arrival of my son Amadeus, when I was 26 years old. At that time, I was surviving a marital betrayal and struggling with postpartum depression. Depression that lasted more than two years—where my self-esteem and my value as a woman had been destroyed. I confess it was an extremely difficult time. On the outside, I wanted to be the perfect mother, but on the inside my world had been trampled, humiliated and betrayed. I had never felt like that, so beaten down and with no will to live. I lost my job, and with that I faced financial failures, but, above all, I lost my dignity and my confidence.

As time went on, I began my personal, mental and spiritual healing process along with my son's growth. The years were slow, but my emotional recovery was getting stronger and stronger. I want to thank my mother who was always in front, my grandfather Zamora who listened attentively to my feelings, his wise words were the perfect guides to not give up and always continue. I always visualized him as an "Oak" symbolically referring to that person with great strength, now my "Oak" is watching over me from heaven.

Amadeus grew more and more, and with his innocence, he showed me the purest and most unconditional love. I learned to be a mother and his friend at the same time. With his wise words he awakened in me every day an enormous interest to grow as a person, being for him an example of a mother, he pushed me and motivated me so much that today I feel very proud of him. Thank you, Amadeus! For being that son, who dried my tears by telling me over and over again-*I believe in you*. And so that's how I recovered my self-respect, but above all my self-esteem.

ONE MORE STROKE OF LIFE

At the age of 32, my life took another turn. Now professionally. I always say that it threw me into the ring, an expression to demonstrate and put into practice what I had learned. The human resources corporate I worked for asked me to sign my resignation letter. This was terrible for me, as it was my only income to support the expenses of my little Amadeus. I thought, my God, how am I going to live, without the steady income of a salary?

I felt anguished and paralyzed, when I checked my purse and realized that all I had was $200 pesos, which I knew was for that day's food. But what about the other days? With a lump in my throat, I accepted the decision that there was no other option. I put my things away from my desk with sadness, I said goodbye to those friends who supported me professionally and emotionally so much. Chris de la Torre and Gloria Sereno, whom I thank with all my heart. I didn't stop feeling injustice about myself from what happened, but even with all this I said to myself, "Easy Xilta, the show must go on. "I thanked them, closed the door and took with me all that I had learned—the confidence, strength and leadership I had developed over these 5 years.

At that time, the COVID-19 pandemic began in Mexico. Between the panic of the virus, my unjustified dismissal, my economic pressures, not having a monetary income in the midst of chaos and uncertainty, fear wanted to take hold of me. But at the same time, an immense desire to take action. I kept repeating to myself, "What am I going to do? while in my mind and heart I had the image of my son.

When asked again, my mind responded, "Sell! "But what am I selling if we are in a pandemic, I answered myself. I searched here and there, and asked so much that I finally saw a glimmer of light that illuminated my face of faith and hope. I knew I had things of value with little use and that maybe other people could use them, so I decided to go out and sell everything I knew could help me momentarily. I offered my psychological therapy services in exchange for food. I had to do what I needed to do. Helping my family and other people in a state of vulnerability, I did food and book deliverer activities and offered red wine through social networks. Despite these circumstances, every morning I thanked and trusted—in God, in the universe and in myself—for having health and the strength to not let myself give up. I discovered that living in victimhood is not the best option, that no matter how you feel, no matter how dark the day is, never lose faith and the firmness and conviction of your dreams.

THE IMPORTANCE OF BELIEVING IN ME

I put on my personal layer of superpowers and connected my heart and mind, creating a synergy of balance that allowed me to take firm steps. Believe me, when you generate that connection in your life you will emerge victorious from all personal challenges, gaining the satisfaction of having believed in yourself. Many people ask me, how do you achieve this magnificent connection? I ask you right now: Have you ever felt in the middle of a decision an inner voice telling you and guiding you, but your mind argues otherwise?

Well, right at that moment is when you must listen to your inner voice. Don't limit it and use its power and execute with your mind. Enjoy the magic that happens when you balance mind and heart, the last thing you need is fear and low confidence! Unleash that power that comes from within you, that magic that binds bits of you together and transforms you to face with resilience.

In 2020 and in the midst of the chaos my life was transformed. I decided to become an entrepreneur. I started as a freelancer offering human resources and psychological therapy services, and I made a list of everything I could do according to my personal qualities—my skills, areas of opportunity and strengths—based on my experience. My surprise was to see the great possibilities I had to start my Human Capital consultancy where I would provide recruitment and selection services, courses, workshops, psychological counseling to companies' personnel.

They say that a hungry stomach, an empty wallet and a broken heart can teach the best life lessons. Today, I, Amaranta Gaytán, can assure you that this is true. These three factors have been my most important challenges that today have shaped me as a person and my profession. Remember: "When you doubt yourself just remember how far you have come, everything you have faced, all the battles you have won and all the fears you have overcome."

It's not always easy though because fears and mental limitations are always looming out the window. It's valid to observe them and feel them, but don't be paralyzed—don't let them consume you—face them! Dare to dream big! It will be inevitable not to have failures and want to give up, but give yourself permission to make mistakes, do not feel guilty for what does not go well, because everything, absolutely everything, comes to teach you and you to learn. Trust yourself and your abilities!

A BRIGHT FUTURE

Today, being 35 years old and writing my story made the little girl inside me feel satisfied with the woman she decided to be. I turned my pain into strength, overcoming adversity with love and courage, calling it *The Magic of Resilience*.

Since this book, I feel different. I feel proud and powerful, but most of all deserving of all that I have received from connecting with women all over the world. Before I begin this new stage, I want to thank Jacqueline Camacho-Ruiz forever. Thank you, Pilotina, for opening my wings! For your infinite MAGIX. Thank you for showing me how wonderful life can be, but most of all for trusting me.

I thank my parents also for their unconditional love. Their lessons and love have taken me far. To my son Amadeus, who has always motivated my steps and makes me grow in me. Thanks to each and every person who has touched my heart and soul. Thank you, Adrian Raymundo, my favorite traveler for being my companion and for bringing out the best in me with your love. I also thank those who have left my life for those who are still by my side trusting me, accompanying and supporting me. THANK YOU!

Now, more than ever, I feel the magic of knowing myself. When I think about the future, I get excited and I know that I am capable of doing everything I set my mind to. I have a lot of hope, new projects in mind and new dreams to fulfill. May the magic continue!

REFLECTION QUESTIONS

1. At what times in your life have you had to be resilient?

2. What qualities and skills make you unique?

3. How can you keep going despite the obstacles you face?

BIOGRAPHY

Amaranta Gaytán is a Psychologist, Mentor, Speaker and Trainer specialized in Human Talent. Amaranta has motivated and trained talents through a strategic approach oriented to human talent, with mastery of techniques in the organizational and clinical area. With extensive communication skills, assertiveness, and empathy, Amaranta is also an expert in hard and soft skills and emotional intelligence.

Amaranta studied at the University of Galilee where she received her B.A. in Clinical Psychology. She has received several diplomas in Management Skills and Emotional Intelligence. In 2021, Amaranta received three certifications for her excellent expertise in human resources.

Currently, she is a Lead Consultant at AtrAm Consultancy where she offers various services to companies and institutions with the objective of achieving an adequate emotional management of workers, stress prevention, time management and customer service. She has also worked as a Senior Recruiter at Adecco where she acted as the world's leading organization in Human Resources, sales and management of recruitment and selection services.

Amaranta Gaytan
IG: @amaranta_
psic.amarantagaytan@gmail.com

PIECES OF ME

Sally Delgado, M.Ed.

"I survived because the fire inside me burned brighter than the fire around me." Joshua Graham

Are you, my Mother? Is a children's book by P.D Eastman that I read to Elijah, my only son, when he was a baby. One of my many tender moments with him that I replay in my memory. I spent most of my childhood wondering if my mother was ever thinking about me, if I resembled her face or her character, and if I would ever get to see her again. Now a mother myself, I found myself wondering more about her and if she would ever get the opportunity to meet her grandson. When I was two years old, my father took primary custody of both me and my eldest sibling after my mother forfeited her rights to parent us both. My father and eldest sister had attempted to find her many times over the years, and each time we were closer to locating her whereabouts in Puerto Rico where she was last seen by relatives. We would drive up and down mountain roads in Puerto Rico asking around the streets for her and each time we located other relatives. Over the years we made several trips to the island and attempted to locate her once again but always fell short. Then during another attempt when I was about twelve years old, we received news that she was staying with family and went to the address nearby. I imagined that she would be overjoyed to see us and reestablish contact. As we drove up the dirt road, I could hardly contain myself, and gathered my gifts that we had made and brought for her. But our visit was nothing more than traumatizing. She was sitting in a rocking chair on the patio when she realized who we were and chucked the Pepsi she was drinking into the ground. I was so confused, as you can imagine, and my eldest sister began crying. I was disappointed. We had come all this way to visit her and that's the welcome we got.

Another thirty years would pass by before getting the phone call that I never thought I would get. Recently, my relatives had found me on social media promoting real estate classes and called the number to inform me that my mother was not well and did not have much longer to live. The hospital was seeking next kin to ultimately decide on her fate. I immediately called my sister, to inform her that I had found our mother's whereabouts and that she wasn't well, and we didn't have much time to figure things out. The pandemic hindered my visit to see her one last time, but my eldest sister was able to be by her side. All these years I waited and wondered, only to find her on her death bed.

A VISIT FROM SATAN

I was asleep on a hot summer evening. My son next to me and the air conditioner that I had told the landlord to fix so many times before continued to drip. At night, you could see the under-door glare of the hallway lights in the building, but not tonight. I was awakened to what I thought was an intruder in my house and became filled with fear and panic to get to my son. But I couldn't move. A force was holding me down heavy, pulling my hair back until my head couldn't be stretched further. The air conditioner in the living room was flickering on and off like straight out of the movie *Poltergeist* and I reached behind me to fight when I realized no one was behind me. I started to pray aloud, and I saw this smog of black air escape the room, then the glare under the door returned. I continued to pray and didn't stop until I felt my hair let loose and ran to see if my son was okay. Unharmed, I continued to pray throughout the night and realized that Satan had come to visit me. It was a fair attempt to see if I would collapse into his misery, since it was the most venerable time in my life. A failed mission indeed. I am a child of God, and nothing can withstand his love for me.

THE COWARDLY LION

I met a guy. I thought he was the greatest until my nightmare began. He called me a cunt, a bitch, and spit in my face countless times. He even thought it would be a good idea to take my son away from me, until I got an order of protection against him and had the SWAT team retrieve my son. He said I was an unfit mother, crashed into my car while driving, he attempted to instill fear in me, stole my time, my trust, my money, and my peace. I never gave his words power, so they never had any meaning. I forgave him, so I could flourish. I just picked up my stuff one day and left his sorry ass with my name and dignity intact.

LATINA RISE

I had the hopes of going to an ivy league University like Yale, Princeton, or Harvard and being on the rowing team. Given the right circumstances I probably would have excelled further and done very well for myself. But life had other plans for me. I walked away from a job opportunity after working so hard to earn it in the first place and decided instead to enroll into Wilbur Wright Community College at twenty-eight years old. I knew nothing before walking into this journey, I simply had the belief that I was in the right place at the right time. Navigating college was difficult at first since no one in my family had mastered it before. But I asked a lot of questions along the way, relentlessly meeting with my advisors and the Financial Aid office. I even got involved in campus activities. I excelled in my studies and breezed through my first two years with honors. Then, I transferred to Northeastern Illinois University (NEIU), and by the time I started my graduate program at DePaul University I was ahead of the class, starting assignments before they were due and reading scholarly articles in advance. I fell in love with learning and excelled at it. Ultimately, I graduated with distinctions. Making this one important decision in my life made all the difference towards everything I wanted to accomplish. The value of listening to your heart and intuition are invaluable.

LOS CONSEJOS DE PAPI

My father is the eldest of nine siblings. Most of them have long passed away from substance abuse and failed health issues.

So, as you can imagine my father experienced a lot of grief and adversity growing up and much throughout his life especially raising both myself and my eldest sibling on his own. There's a certain kind of rhetoric that every Latino father comes equipped with, mine came with double ammunition, for the next nineteen years of my life. A life filled with restrictions, parables, stories, and warnings. It was a constant in the house—

"Turn off the lights"
"Hang up the phone"
"There's no money for that!"
"You're not going anywhere"
"Those shorts are too short"
"Turn down the music"
"Be back on time or else"
"Who didn't do the dishes?"

Especially when he picked up the phone line to listen in on my conversations when boys called me. As if I couldn't hear his heavy breathing on the other end. Growing up, my dad devoted his time to taking us to the zoo, museums, and parks. I remember so many times going to the lake and picnicking on the sand. I loved to see the Chicago skyline and the famous Playboy Mansion at the Palmolive building, with the lit up bunny at night. I would always tell my dad I wanted to work there, he always thought that was funny. Then I learned why years later. My father gave his best in raising us. He made mistakes, a lot of them, but he ultimately could only give what he had in his love bank. My existence required gallons of love, praise, and affection when he only came equipped with pint sizes. I could never hold my father accountable for the absence of my mother or the shortcomings of his own childhood. I understood that early on. I was just thankful that I still had one awesome parent to carry the torch.

BIONIC WOMAN

My dad had always wanted a boy. He finally got one after four girls but before he got his wish my sister and I got recruited to serve as professional movers, mechanics, and handymen. We hated it passionately. I still don't know the difference between a screwdriver or pilers. One time my dad needed us to hold a sheet of drywall up to the ceiling while he drilled it down, my arms were shaking after he was taking his time measuring and taking sips of his coffee; I yelled *"I can't anymore,"* and the wall collapsed onto our heads leaving us covered in white powered chalk. We moved around a lot when I was young. I even went to about six preparatory schools before settling into 4th grade. Each time we moved it was dreadful. Boxes, tape, and helping to load up heavy furniture sometimes from the third-floor apartment. He even went as far as purchasing moving dollies and those ridiculous moving belts to strap around your waistline so that we could carry heavy items. My sister and I carried sofas, stoves, refrigerators, and beds down flights of stairs like true professionals.

THE ROAD TO CHARACTER

Today, I embrace and celebrate all my flaws, failures, losses, and even my father's advice. These experiences have molded me into the person I am today and have evoked within me the desire to inspire and impact on an unimaginable level. I had navigated life through unfortunate circumstances and believe that they all had to occur for me to find the road to character. It took years for me to forgive those that brought harm and disappointment to my life, but it was necessary so that I could grow. I regret nothing.

REFLECTION QUESTIONS

1. How has your childhood impacted your career choices?

2. What was the best/worst advice your parents gave you growing up?

3. What lessons did you take away after overcoming adversity?

BIOGRAPHY

Sally Delgado is the newly appointed Vice President of Operations at Realty of Chicago [ROC], a thriving brokerage firm with five locations, award-winning distinctions and recognitions, and a growing roster of over 300 agents to date. Prior to her appointment, Sally served as an educator with over a decade of experience in education ranging from non-profit organizations, post-secondary, and higher education. Sally leads with confidence, a solution-focused mindset and has an unmatched track record of achievements. Her innate ability to connect with people and her energy set her apart.

Sally is an alumna of DePaul University, where she was recognized for the *Latino Student Leadership Award* among her peers. She is an alumna of Mujeres de HACE cohort 2020, an ambassador for St. Jude Children Research Hospital, and served on the Casa Central Auxiliary ELAB board. Sally is looking forward to amplifying the Realty of Chicago brand and strategic development while bolstering the broker and clientele experience.

Sally Delgado, M.Ed.
Sally@realtyofchicago.com
Facebook: Facebook.com/sallydelgado
LinkedIn: www.linkedin.com/in/
sallydelgadorocsold

Lorena Rebeca Beltrán González

"An an ordinary pen is better than a prodigious mind; they give shape to dreams and visions even in the storm."

With this quote in mind, I managed to understand how important it is to capture my story, so that more women could take it as inspiration and an impulse in this life full of obstacles, to undoubtedly give us courage to face on and continue—but above all to continue transcending.

I am Lorena Rebeca Beltrán González, originally from beautiful Puerto Vallarta, Jalisco, Mexico. *"The friendliest city in the world."* From a very young age I heard these words from my parents who have dedicated their lives to service and tourism, the top source of income of my beautiful Puerto Vallarta. From my parents I learned the love of service and the courage to carry on a legacy that today more than ever I treasure. I love where I was sown and today, I bear fruit.

I came into this world in a traditional family. My father, Francisco Beltrán López, was a pioneer in the tourism industry.

My mother, Rebeca González Aréchiga, was a housewife. A woman who undoubtedly has been a great example for me of not giving up and moving forward. I have two siblings, Adriana and Paco, whom I thank from the bottom of my heart for all their support, love, but above all the respect they give me.

I got married young at the age of 20 with my boyfriend of six years, my only and my great love, Carlo Iván Gómez Pérez. Yes, when I say my only great love, it is because I met him in high school, two young people with the desire to form a family. And great family we formed as we were able to bring to the world 4 beautiful children—two women and two men—an army! Today, Carlo Iván is 25 years old, Carolina Isabel is 23 years old, Diego Emanuel is 20 years old and the youngest of the family, Ana Lorena is 18 years old. You can imagine how I would split myself in two as most are only 2 years apart! But how I thank God for these special moments.

Nonetheless, I thought I was going crazy when my personal dreams were slipping away as I entered this new phase of building our family. I remember that even when I was pregnant, I was attending college with the faithful purpose of fulfilling my goals and dreams, but what a surprise! I felt that my struggle was becoming more and more difficult as I listened to the opinions of others such as: "The woman should be at home taking care of her husband, why did you get married, why do you have children, you're a fool you won't make it!" The judgments were great and came from a harsh society. I hated to hear and see that I was part of a repetitive statistic as I was a young mom. My life partner also had dreams and seeing that he was the breadwinner at that time it was crucial to give in to the situation. In my mind, I was struck by this internal struggle of POWER that pretended to give no truce, without knowing that the man I had by my side was a passionate leader who needed to be supported.

SOMEONE HAS TO GIVE IN

Yes... it had to be me! At such a crossroads I gave in to loving my role as a mother, to being that woman as who ran a tight ship but cared for her crew. I invite you to read Proverbs 31:14, as it shares a very powerful lesson.

I discovered and decided that this would be my best life project! My house, the raising of my children, the best partner for my husband. However, it is worth mentioning that my parents had decided to end their marriage. At a time when it was heavily criticized to come from a broken family, there were times when I was bullied at the Catholic school where I studied. One day I asked my mother why my father was leaving home. She answered my question by saying, **"It is better to have peace than to be right!"** With these simple words I could understand at my young age the power to face this new feeling that was pressuring me to believe in never divorcing. I decided to put these thoughts behind as it was a generational chain and not welcome here. I wanted to live my life and my future relationship in a certain way and I had it in my mind that I would make it! Yet, to this day I am still fighting. I realized that there is no such thing as a perfect man or woman, only two imperfect partners. In my own relationship, I watched my partners plans and I was always there. His love was not selfish, on the contrary, we knew it was a long-term decision to be together and to grow. For me, it meant giving my all and believing in my own strengths that God allowed me to see when I let him be my guide.

MY GREATEST ALLY

I thank those people who came into my life when I was so young and at a time when I thought everything was going well—my house, my children, my finances. Thank you for being there when I couldn't find myself or when I was asked how I was doing and how I was feeling or how I was managing to keep my balance. Let me tell you that it is one thing to give in and another to give in with purpose. My plan was to dedicate myself to my family and my marriage and work hard for them. But as I very importantly learned, never give up on yourself as a woman. Not physically, not emotionally and certainly not spiritually. It is so important to give place to that which emanates strength and above all that wisdom that is necessary to continue. I went through hard times in my life. One of those difficult moments was when I found out about the infidelity of the only being who was for me; my everything, my friend, my partner, the love of my life, the father of my children. My world really fell apart.

When God came to me, I opened the door of my mind, of my heart and I found a wonderful treasure. I found a beautiful guide that explained to me step by step how to continue walking with faith. He was constant that no matter how many problems

I saw in front of me, it was like a balm that lessened my pain and my state of despair.

Another difficult moment was when one of my sons at the age of 17 suffered a terrible accident where every prognosis was against him. As a mother it was such a horrible experience, but thank God he gave me strength.

Moments that have put us to the test have been when we lost tourist concessions in several parts of the city overnight due to the first pandemic in Mexico, which was the influenza in 2009. But without a doubt the most recent obstacles were with this pandemic and the COVID-19 virus. Like many Latinas, I am a survivor of this horrible disease where fear was stronger than my faith. Along with my husband—who was contaminated first—after three days I began to feel symptoms. We were isolated and the severity started ten days after we were contaminated. We had to be transferred to the hospital because my husband needed oxygen urgently. These were such traumatic moments, but this is when the angels arrived at the door of our house in human form. My brothers and sister-in-law, Guillermo, Fabricio, and Dinora Gomez were my lifeline. Not to mention Hector Ventura, the best friend of the family. Also a great woman who has been a synodal in my life, a true example of integrity and dedication to her children—who through prayer led me to have an unwavering faith—my mother-in-law and mentor Isabel Gomez, to them many thanks.

Through time, I was able to forgive, love, thank and continue my life in spite of everything I have been through. I was able to appreciate that everything that happened would sooner or later bring a reward that would return each of the pieces of my life that had been stolen. I will never stop teaching my children that faith is our only way to continue on in this life. As the seconds go by, it's still complex to live in this world, but everything can be overcome with faith.

Forgiveness is the weapon and shield that did not let guilt and hatred take position in my life. That is why I continue to fight day by day, every day reminding myself that I am a capable woman and I thank God for the opportunity that He has given me to learn. I know that time and time again the tests were enough to raise my pride and defend my home and my family because no one else would do it. That someone had to give in for victory to take its place and that justice would lead me to be a woman with deep roots. Even if strong winds came I would not fall!

MY PURPOSE

It is a great power to be a woman who transcends. A woman who has left a legacy in my generations, with the strong conviction that family is the best life project. I am a woman who continues to fight for this institution that today more than ever we must fight and be responsible and coherent. But above all with respect and love for others who do not share your purpose in life. May your values continue to be promoted without stepping on anyone's toes. Continue to form words that restart a different course and that do good to the soul. Words that give momentum in these times where alliances create solidity and permanence. Now I can see that times change, everything changes—the clothes, the music, the way of doing business and the family itself. Life has led me to go the extra mile by constantly motivating myself to stay relevant and to cope with my teenage children and business. I am a blessed woman and I know I can do it all!

REFLECTION QUESTIONS

1. What do you need to know to find your purpose?
2. Do you think it is better to work as a team?
3. Is it worth waiting patiently for your turn in the business world?
4. Are you happy with what you have?

BIOGRAPHY

Lorena Beltrán González is a 100% Puerto Vallarta business woman. Together with her husband, they built a family business dedicated to tourism services. Their company, known as Vallarta View Adventures, is located in the bay with a zipline located in the mountains of the city.

Lorena is President of the National Chamber of Small Commerce, Services and Tourism of Puerto Vallarta, Jalisco, Mexico. She is also a National Counselor of the Confederation of National Chambers of Commerce of the Country (Concanaco). Lorena is Founder of the Platform (SICE) Sistema Integral De Capacitación Para el Emprendimiento (Integral Training System For Entrepreneurship).

More recently, Lorena has created together with Jaqueline Camacho Ruiz, a great promoter and entrepreneur, the Impulso 2022 Project, which supports young people with innovative ideas in Puerto Vallarta. Together with Jacqueline, these two businesswomen are helping other businesswomen in Puerto Vallarta to move forward and transcend!

Lorena found that her passion was to work alongside her husband to promote a large group of entrepreneurs and business owners. Through the Chamber of Commerce, which she represents-with sustainable projects and within reach from the smallest entrepreneurs to the most consolidated entrepreneurs-they provide free trainings to empower and guide the entrepreneurs to reach and advance to another level. To date they have impacted more than 3000 entrepreneurs in Puerto Vallarta and in different cities of the country such as Coatzacoalcos, Veracruz, Queretaro and Nayarit.

Lorena Beltran
IG: @lorebg06
lorenabeltran@msn.com

Jacqueline S. Ruíz

**ENTREPRENEUR, AUTHOR, SPEAKER, PILOT,
TODAY'S INSPIRED LATINA FOUNDER**

ABOUT THE AUTHOR

Jacqueline Ruiz is a visionary social entrepreneur that has created an enterprise of inspiration. With more of 20 years of experience in the marketing and Public Relations industry, she has created two successful award-winning companies, established two nonprofit organizations, published 27 books, the largest collection of Latina stories in a book anthology series in the world, and held events in four continents. She has received over 30 awards for her contributions and business acumen.

Jacqueline is currently the CEO of award-winning JJR Marketing, one of the fastest-growing top marketing and public relations agencies in Chicago, and Fig Factor Media, an international media publishing company that helps individuals bring their books to life. Jacqueline is also the Founder of The Fig Factor Foundation, a not-for-profit organization dedicated to giving vision, direction, and structure to young Latinas ages 12-25 as well as the President of Instituto Desarrollo Amazing Aguascalientes, the first youth center in Calvillo, Aguascalientes, Mexico, offering various hands-on experience, courses, and global connections to support the local troubled youth in defining their dreams.

Jacqueline currently serves as a board member for the The Fig Factor Foundation, the Alumni Executive Board at the College of DuPage and the World Leaders Forum. She is a recent graduate of the DePaul University Women Entrepreneurship Cohort 3 and the Stanford University Graduate School of Business, Latino Business Action Network Cohort 11. She represents the 2.6% of women entrepreneurs with over seven figures in the United States. Jacqueline is one of the very few Latina sports airplane pilots in the United States and the founder of Latinas in Aviation global brand that now includes the book, magazine, scholarship and events. She believes that "taking off is optional, landing on your dreams is mandatory."